British Design
2004–2005

Branding and Graphic Design
Packaging Design
New Media Design
Interior, Retail and Event Design
Product Design

BIS Publishers
Herengracht 370-372
1016 CH Amsterdam
P.O. Box 323
1000 AH Amsterdam
The Netherlands
T +31 (0)20 524 7560
F +31 (0)20 524 7557
bis@bispublishers.nl
www.bispublishers.nl

Copyright © 2004 BIS Publishers, Amsterdam

ISBN 90-6369-071-1

British Design
2004–2005

Branding and Graphic Design
Packaging Design
New Media Design
Interior, Retail and Event Design
Product Design

Contents

Design Agencies by Location

01 Ashbourne
Word of

02 Basildon
Mansfields

03 Bath
Osborne Pike

04 Birmingham
Boxer
Fluid
Kiwi
Lunartik
Tibbatts Associates Ltd

05 Braintree
Pocknell Studio

06 Bristol
Taxi Studio Ltd

07 Cheltenham
Hurricane Design Consultants Ltd

08 Chester
Loines Furnival

09 Coventry
Budding

10 Edinburgh
Navyblue Design Group
Zero Design Limited

11 Glasgow
Front Page Design
Red Cell Scotland

12 Halifax
Reinvigorate

13 Hove
Design LSM

14 Leeds
dare!
Watt

15 Leicester
Checkland Kindleysides Ltd

16 London
A.D. Creative Consultants
Alembic Design Consultants
Aukett Limited
automatic
BDP Design
Blackburn's Ltd
Bloom Brand Design
Boxer
Brewer Riddiford Design Consultants
Dalziel and Pow Design Consultants
Design Bridge
Dew Gibbons

Enterprise IG
Etu Odi Design
Fitch
Gensler
Hothouse Product Development Partners
Indigo Partnership International
jones knowles ritchie
Kiwi
Lloyd Northover
Minx Creative
MoreySmith
David Morgan Associates
Navyblue Design Group
The Nest
Odd
OPX
Oyster Partners Ltd
PDD
R Design
Seachange Creative Partners
Spin
Springetts
Start Creative Limited
Two by Two

17 Long Compton
Arapaho Communications Limited

18 Manchester
Hemisphere Design & Marketing Consultants
Studio North

19 Marlborough
Tin Horse

20 Moira
IDa

21 Newcastle (including Gateshead)
Beacon Creative Ltd
Blue River
FUSEBOXDESIGN Ltd
Infinite Design

22 Norwich
Product Resolutions Ltd

23 Nottingham
cl design
Pure
Philip Watts Design

24 Richmond-upon-Thames
Landesign

25 Truro
Creative Edge

26 Windsor
Oliis Design

Foreword

Welcome to *British Design 2004-2005*, the second edition of BIS Publishers' cross-section of design studios and creative consultancies in Britain. We are proud to offer the British creative industry and its domestic and international clients this completely new, second survey of creative talent from the UK. The changes in the design industry over the last two years is of course reflected in this book: a lot of new names now present themselves for the first time, along with many established firms that are in here again because they experienced the benefits of getting their work out to the (inter)national audience of design buyers who use the book.

The goal of this book is simple: it helps clients in their search for the ideal design partner. *British Design 2004-2005* provides an instant impression of each participating studio's work – it is a reference tool for whenever professional creative input is needed.

To underestimate the power of design as a visual communication interface between user and product would be a grave error in judgement. This is the conclusion of Corinna Dean's article in this book. Look around you and you see a world full of identities, trademarks and other interfaces. It is apparent that the commercial world is aware of the necessity of working with design. The new challenge however, for both clients and designers, is to really differentiate through creativity, to become a first grade version of yourself, rather than a second grade version of somebody else. Keep that in mind when you talk with one of the fine agencies in this book.

Rudolf van Wezel
BIS Publishers

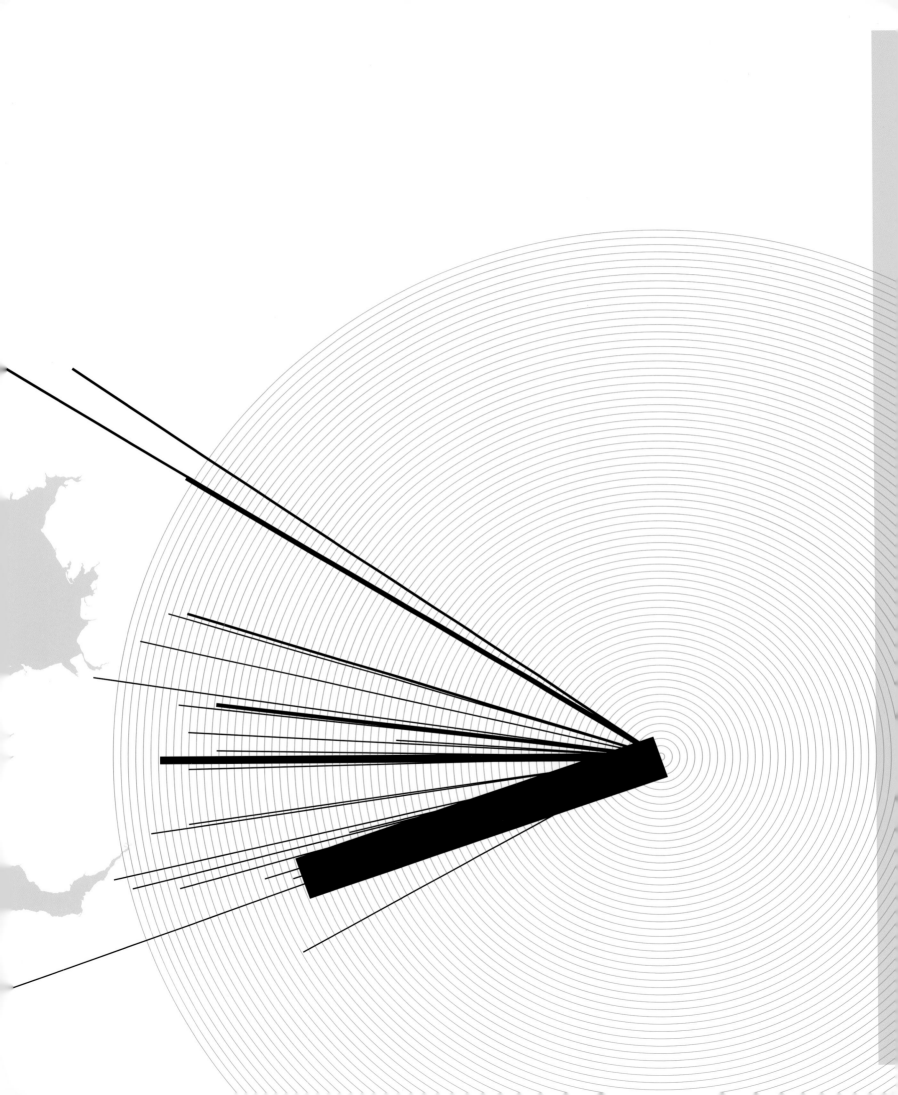

Design and Business:
Does Design make a Difference to Business?

By Corrina Dean

Cast one's mind back to the Eighties, the decade of excess, with a market saturated in designer objects. Satirically portrayed in the Hollywood film, *Wall Street*, the epitome of yuppie greed, indulgence and designer "must-haves", the film's telling scene sums up the mood of the Eighties: Bud Fox, the Wall Street dealer and his father, played by Martin Sheen, sit in Bud's penthouse apartment, kitted out with high-tech designer furniture, against a Manhattan skyline. Sheen places his books on the glass coffee table, detailed with a large crevice running through its centre. The books fall through the crevice, an example of function, that Modernist dictum, truly lost to the frivolities of style. And so it continued, designer lemon squeezers, such as Philippe Starck's Juicy Salif, which looked good, but it didn't really matter if the juice trickled unstylishly down one of the four elegant legs.

Moving into the Nineties, a more sophisticated tone was struck with the launch of *Wallpaper**. The magazine's editor, Tyler Brule, former war correspondent turned lifestyle guru, created a whole new level of aspirational living. *Wallpaper's* heady interior spreads meant that telling the design story often took a back seat: What are design's values today and what can good design contribute to culture and commerce?

An early twentieth-century example of commerce waking up to the benefits of engaging designers was the leading German electrical company, AEG, in their appointment of the architect and industrial designer, Peter Behrens. Behrens joined the *Allgemeine Elektricitätsgesellschaft* in 1907 and acted as a design consultant for everything that AEG built,

manufactured or printed. In the drive for German industry to compete on the European market, wherever German industries set up retail ventures, they soon employed the services of designers. At the same time, Hermann Muthesius founded the *Deutscher Werkbund*, a design foundation funded by the Weimar Republic to promote good design and architecture. The two events marked a new relationship between creative designers and industry.

Product and Retail Design

Moving through the twentieth century, other seminal examples of design and commerce shine as beacons to the success of engaging designers with business. After the American Depression, manufacturers of hard goods, such as washing machines, cameras and electrical goods, needed to give their products a boost on the flagging market. A new breed of designers, some trained as advertising draughtsmen, were brought in as the first generation of consultant industrial designers, one of them being the ubiquitous designer Raymond Loewy, probably best known for his design of the Lucky Strike cigarette packet designed in the 1940s, which has become an icon of American culture. Loewy went on to design the Greyhound Bus and many other products, creating a style that established a mass aesthetic.

If one were to select one company which has systematically built up their reputation of uncompromising products designed around the principles of function, then Braun, the household appliance firm established in 1951, springs to mind. Braun has become a by-word for "good design", and the company's track record of employing such respected designers

as Dieter Rams is legendary. Rams has been credited with developing an aesthetic that has become the epitome of Germany's economic miracle. Braun's influence has been widespread.

Rowenta, the French appliance company, recently engaged Jasper Morrison, one of Britain's leading product designers, to redesign their appliance range. The forms and detailing can be viewed as directly descendent from the work of Rams. Braun's history reflects one of the earliest examples of brand building. Through the company's early appreciation of design, a strong brand has developed.

Just over a decade since Jonathan Ive joined Apple Mac, there has been a seismic shift in the consumer's relationship to computing. The beige box has been scrapped and in its place is a product semantic that reflects the creativity of 3-D graphics and technology. Ive, together with the Apple Mac's founder Steve Jobs, has collaborated to produce a range of products that continue to rethink and reshape how we use computer interfaces. As Vice President of Industrial Design for Apple, Ive and his design team play a central role in the company's development. Focus groups are abhorred and a product's development is largely in the hands of the design team. An example of Ive's astute ability to steer the market is epitomised in his design of the covetable i-Pod. The product took the function of the MP-3 player, largely a tool targeted at "techies", and brought the technology to a far larger audience. As a result of the product's success, Apple launched its own iTunes software store, an online record shop which contains 2,000,000 songs at 99 cents apiece.

Turning to the glittering world of retail and fashion, there is a marked increase in the number of boutiques on the high street. Adam Brinkworth's retail design for the high street store, Karen Miller, has brought a degree of minimal sophistication that reflects the merchandise. Fashion designer Alexander McQueen, backed by the luxury goods company, Gucci, has opened stores in London, Milan and New York, all designed by William Russell. The belief in McQueen by his backers to succeed as a global brand is reflected in their long-term commitment to open fifteen stores worldwide.

Logos and Identity

No one can have failed to be affected by the multitude of design symbols that we are bombarded with within the urban fabric of our cities. Logos communicate subtle, adverse, oblique or overt meanings. Logos are interpreted, reinterpreted, appropriated and counterfeited. To build up a brand identity through the services of a designer is vital. One such early example of the design of a corporate identity and one of the most recognised in Britain, or at least in London, is the London Transport Logo, the bold circle with a line through its centre. Frank Pick, the commercial manager of London Transport, commissioned one of the most thorough corporate identity schemes by employing the architect Charles Holden and the typographer Edward Johnston to create a unified appearance for the system, still in use today.

Witness the Nike swoosh, a symbol as recognised worldwide as the United States dollar sign or the ubiquitous Louis Vuitton logo made infamous by footballer's wives. One of Britain's leading design consultancies in the Nineties, Wolf Ollins, demonstrated a canniness in predicting a new field of brand identity. They realised that this process could be applied to the branding of countries. A research document for the British government's think tank, The Foreign Policy Centre, resulted in the television documentary, *Made in Britain*. Perhaps an early example of spin, the government realised that design identity was a useful tool to succinctly present a positive view of the nation. The success of the design consultancy in awakening the government to how they could influence the projection of the country's image through design and branding techniques was prophetic. A pamphlet was produced by the British Tourist Board, titled *Branding Britain* (1997), and this coincided with the emergence of the "Cool Britannia" [label and the rest is history] slogan.

Publicity

In a recent survey that mapped Britain's response to advertising, four camps were identified. Out of those four, the largest group, making up thirty-five percent, were identified as The Enthusiasts – those who can't get enough advertising. Their tastes were classified as preferring ads and commercials which were filled with intrigue. It wouldn't be over-hyping the medium to label advertising as a universally recognised art form. With this cultural definition, it is hard to ignore the power that publicity can have in influencing the consumer. Love it or loathe it, the FCUK campaign, for example, has brought phenomenal success to the retailer, French Connection. With its mix of controversy and admiration, the advertising campaign, with its simple word play, has contributed to the company's ongoing success.

New Media

As predictions forecasted, the rise of the Internet has had an enormous influence on not only the creative industries, but in the increase of access to services and products. Airside, the London-based new media and print design company, have an impressive client list that ranges from the White Cube Gallery to Chanel. The company's off-beat graphic style,

accompanied by their ability to transcend into other creative fields – Airside's director is also a partner of the successful techno-indie band, Lemonjelly – means that a certain street cred is brought to their work.

As creative parameters are expanded with the increasing possibilities of technology, a new classification of designer is emerging. Daniel Brown, winner of the Design Museum's Designer of the Year 2004 award, describes himself as a Creative Technologist in the field of digital and interactive design. His creative expertise, combined with technological knowledge, means that he is in great demand from companies keen to demonstrate their position at the edge of new technological developments. Sony Playstation hired Brown for their Third Place interactive website, as well as for Play/Create, an interactive video track label which releases new media projects.

To underestimate the power of design as a visual communication interface between user and product would amount to a grave omission. The commissioning of a design agency brings a unique creative process which seeks to understand the desires of the client and to promote and communicate those desires. A design company brings not only professional expertise, but an original eye and creative energy essential for a company's on-going success.

Alembic Design Consultants
Communications Design

1 Hanover Yard / Noel Road / London N1 8YA
T +44 (0)20 7288 4580 / T +44 (0)7973 416261
jmiller@alembic.co.uk
www.alembic.co.uk

Contact Jonathan Miller
Founded 1995

Company Profile
Alembic is an independent design consultancy specialising in clear and effective communications design.

Equally committed to both creativity and client needs, the Alembic approach is characterised by careful distillation of essential information, an emphasis on substance and structure as well as surface; and awareness of project context, timing and cost.

Alembic works on both long-term strategic projects and smaller scale one-off communications with clients of all kinds, from small charities to large public companies.

Typical projects include annual reports and corporate literature, environmental graphics, marketing communications and on-screen design.

Alembic also has considerable experience of creating new visual identities for corporate and consumer brands, and particular expertise in developing strategies to evolve, implement and manage existing brands.

Clients
Asset Value Investors
Ceema Technology
CS Healthcare
Datamonitor
Eurosport
Financial Publishing International
First Islamic Investment Bank
Fletcher Priest Architects
Granada Media
Merrill Lynch Europe
Mount Alvernia Hospital
Petrogal
Portugal Telecom
Sport England
The Film Editors
Tindall Riley
Villeroy & Boch

1 Annual report (part 1), Sport England, 2002
2 Annual report (part 2), Sport England, 2002
3 Brand identity, Spencer Music, 2002
4 Visual identity development, Virtuall, 2003
5 Cashplan health insurance brand identity,
  CS Healthcare, 2002
6 Wayfinding graphic, Fletcher Priest Architects, 2000
7 Website, Hamilton Billiards, 2002
8 Brand identity & product literature,
  Fresh Bathrooms, 2003

1

2

3

4

7

CP **Plus**

5

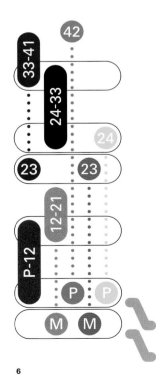

6

8

Arapaho Communications Limited
Arapaho Design, Accrue* Corporate Reporting

Parson's Barn / Main Street / Long Compton
Warwickshire CV36 5LJ
T +44 (0)1608 684 841 / F +44 (0)1608 684 849
in²o@arapaho.co.uk
www.arapaho.co.uk

Accrue* Corporate Reporting / 282 Waterloo Road
London SE1 8RQ
T +44 (0)20 7902 7277 / F +44 (0)20 7928 5136
corporate.reporting@accrue.info
www.accrue.info

Management Richard Guy **Contact** Richard Guy
Staff 6 **Founded** 1983

Arapaho

Arapaho's full design service includes literature, corporate identity, advertising, exhibitions, packaging and online communications. We have in-house design, production, copywriting and project management skills. These can be supplemented by our established working relationships with a variety of specialists.

We take care to develop an understanding of your business and go on to build a partnership in which you'll work directly with our designers. This, combined with our 'can do' attitude, ensures that our creative solutions really do fit your needs and are delivered on time and to brief.

The 2004 Design Week Top 100 survey ranked us at No.7 for productivity, which means we also offer excellent value.

Clients include
Capital One
Experian
Freestyle New Media
GUS
Industrious

Accrue* Corporate Reporting

A subsidiary to Arapaho, Accrue concentrates on the specialised field of corporate reporting. We are familiar with the issues of diverse stakeholder groups, CSR, governance codes and online delivery.

We work with you as an extension of your team, whether you require an annual report or a complete investor reporting service.

Our core service is based on creative direction and project management with design, copywriting and production expertise. Where necessary, we can add the expertise of strategic partners in associated disciplines, orchestrating the various processes and skills to supply you with a seamless service.

Clients include
AEA Technology
Birmingham City FC
GUS
Imprima de Bussy
Jarvis Porter Group
Tribal Group

Images taken from the GUS annual report 2004, created by Accrue* Corporate Reporting

The new Burberry store in Milan was the first in Italy and another milestone for the brand

The new 60,000 square metre central distribution centre in Barton is part of a £120m investment in the Argos supply chain

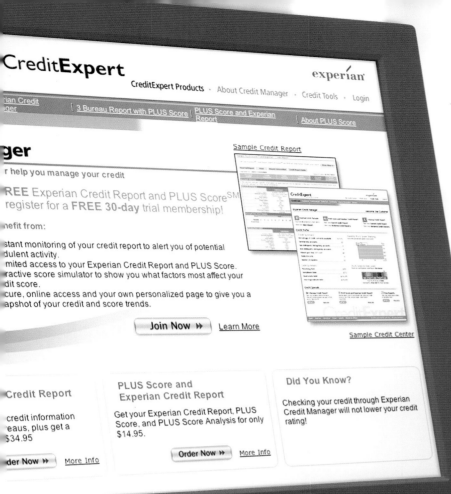

"We believe that the best design and creative work is driven by passion for our business and a genuine 'can-do' attitude"

automatic

Top Floor / 100 De Beauvoir Road / London N1 4EN
T +44 (0)20 7923 4857
speak@automatic-design.com
www.automatic-design.com

Management Martin Carty, Ben Tibbs
Contacts Martin Carty, Ben Tibbs
Staff 3 **Founded** 1995

1 Cross-media campaign with 4Creative, for 'Indian Summer' – a season of programmes, events and live Test Match cricket. The fluid visual language is partly inspired by coloured pigment throwing during the Hindu 'Holi' Festival. 4Creative/Channel 4

2 Theatre brochure for Laban – one of Europe's leading institutions for contemporary dance artist training. As part of evolving the new visual identity, we treated the 2D spaces of the covers and posters as 'empty white performance spaces' in which to place abstracted images of the performers. Laban

3 Mailer for 'Turner Prize and Contemporary Arts Practice' course – an initiative for Artist/Teachers. Inspired by the ideas of debate, reflection and new growth, we created a design featuring a 'thinking chair', a eucalyptus tree and paint dribbles. Tate/The London Institute

4 Poster and catalogue for 'Output' – Kingston University Faculty of Art, Design and Music Degree Show, 2003. The concept revolves around the use of a series of two-syllable instructions. Kingston University

5 Posters for 'Exposure' – Kingston University Faculty of Art, Design and Music Degree Show, 2002. With a theme of 'making the unseen seen', we used photographic images of 3D objects that we'd deconstructed to reveal their abstract, flat forms. Kingston University

6 Coffee shop identity from an exploratory branding project. Exploring the informal, 'spoken' nature of the brand name. BDG McColl

7 Identity for the photographic agency FIRE, inspired by the reversed text on the front of fire engines. FIRE

8 Entry pack for the Young at Art Awards, 2004 – a scheme recognising imaginative and creative practice in schools across Greater London. Each of the 32 postcards contains eclectic combinations of inspirational starting points, unusual raw materials and images of randomly collected equipment. The London Institute

9 Folded catalogue for 'Athens-scape' at the Royal Institute of British Architects – an exhibition exploring the transformation of the City of Athens in the run-up to the 2004 Olympics. The identity and disjointed concertina-fold evolved from grid explorations by Tessera, the exhibition designers. The Hellenic Ministry of Culture

10 Publication for the Royal College of Art to raise awareness and funding for their new building project, The Ellipse, by architects Nicholas Grimshaw & Partners. Contemplating the implications of a brand new, untouched building, we first asked, 'what makes a creative space?' The traces left behind in the college each year – masking tape on desks, names on plan chests, paint splashes around sinks, abandoned work – are physical evidence of the link between 'artist' and 'space', an on-going creative cycle. We wanted any donor to feel that they were investing in this future relationship, rather than just 'a building'. Royal College of Art

11 Panorama – Kingsland Road, London. A multi-purpose architectural guide that can be perforated and re-formed to reveal a 5-metre, continuous panorama of the road itself. The Building Exploratory

Bloom Brand Design

25 The Village / 101 Amies Street / London SW11 2JW
T +44 (0)20 7924 4533 / F +44 (0)20 7924 4553
harriet@bloom-design.com
www.bloom-design.com

Management Gavin Blake, Harriet Marshall, Ben White
Contacts Harriet Marshall, Ben White
Staff 21 **Founded** 2001

Company Profile
Bloom is a compact design agency with three areas
of excellence:
Understanding
Creativity
Delivery

We seek to simplify rather than complicate and we don't
have any black box TM techniques. Our house style is bold,
simple and human, our spirit friendly.

Founded in 2001, we're young, independent and hungry.

Our Clients Include
Associated Newspapers
Danone
Diageo
Disney
Nestle
Spy Publishing
Unilever

See also Packaging Design p. 106

ven

odontics™

Mr & Mrs Smith

Global
Diagnostics

bloom
Brand Design

Blue River

The Foundry / Forth Banks / Newcastle upon Tyne NE1 3PA
T +44 (0)191 261 0000 / F +44 (0)191 261 0010
simon@blueriver.co.uk
www.blueriver.co.uk

Contact Simon Douglas
Staff 11 **Founded** 1996

Blue River works to achieve real results through talent,
hard work and inspired design.

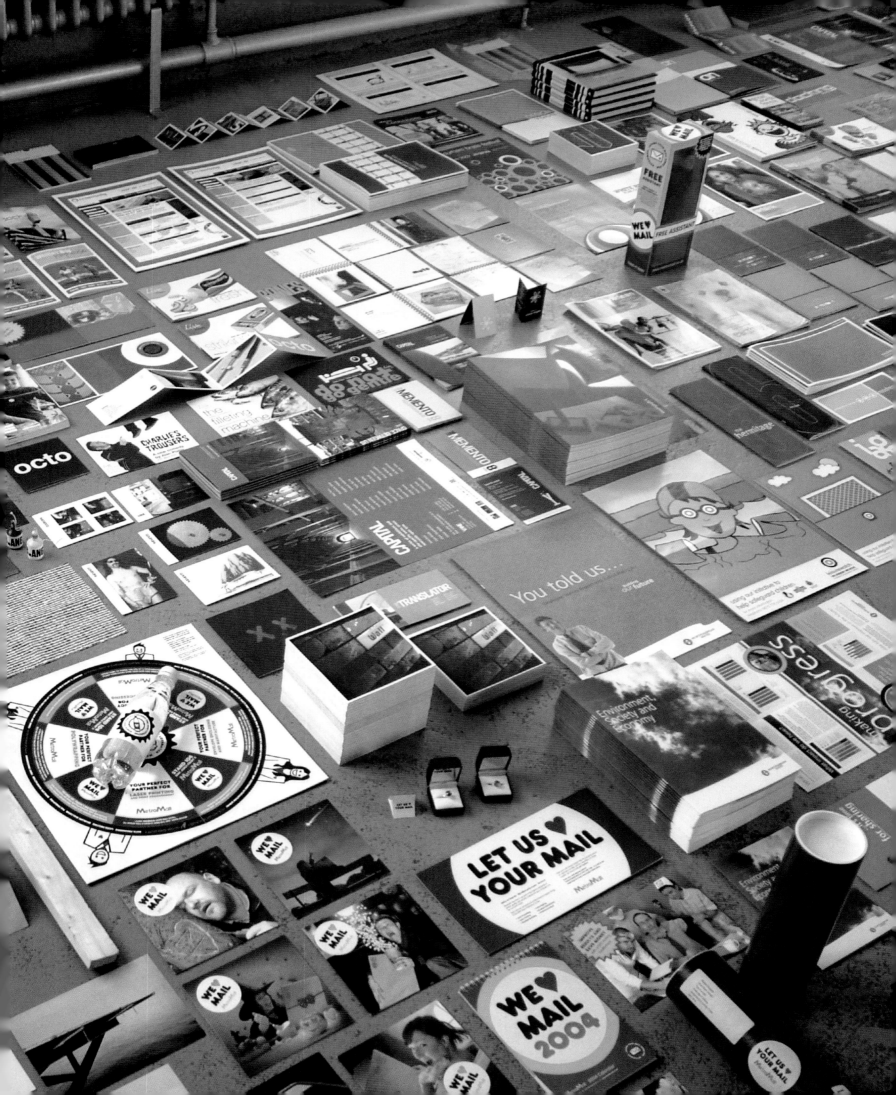

Boxer

St Philip's Court / Church Hill / Coleshill
Birmingham B46 3AD
T +44 (0)1675 467 050 / F +44 (0)1675 465 288
paul@boxer.uk.com
www.boxer.uk.com

Also at: Brand Building / 14 James Street
London WC2E 8BU

See also Packaging Design p. 108

Budding
Creative Design

67 Poplar Road / Earlsdon / Coventry CV5 6FX
T +44 (0)24 7671 4805
info@buddingdesign.com
www.buddingdesign.com

Contact Katy Miranda
Founded 2000

Budding is a creative graphic and web design company.

All our clients are provided with unique original designs to suit their business.

We aim to provide creative and original images in all areas of graphic and web design, through to print.

Our clients offer various services and come from a variety of sectors, including alternative therapies, public services, retail and catering.

1   Eliot's Delivery Service
2   Rocking Horse Kindergarten
3   Buttons for website – 'Lets Rent'
4   Enlighten Your Mind CD covers
5   Website and brochure design for ADECS

ELIOT'S

DELIVERY SERVICE

1

Washing Machine

Parking

Garden

Furnished

Cooker

Shower

Study

Microwave

BE A ROCKING BABY AT THE ROCKING HORSE KINDERGARTEN

2

Budding :Design
image - print - creative - individual

3

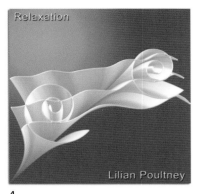
Relaxation
Lilian Poultney

Chakra Meditations
Lilian Poultney

Healing Heart
Lilian Poultney

Earth Mother
Lilian Poultney

4

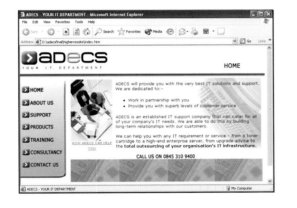

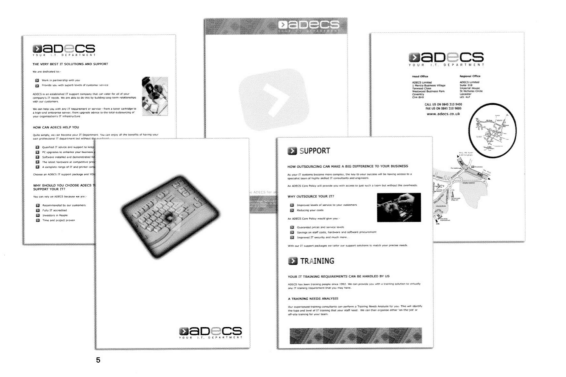

5

Checkland Kindleysides Ltd

Charnwood Edge / Cossington / Leicester LE7 4UZ
Leicestershire
T +44 (0)116 2644 700 / F +44 (0)116 2644 701
marketing@checkind.com
www.checkind.com

Management Jeff Kindleysides, Principal Creative Director
Staff 85 **Founded** 1979

Company Profile
One of the largest independent design consultancies in the
UK and founded in 1979, we celebrate our 25th year in 2004.
We are a multi-disciplined design consultancy which
specialises in engaging consumers through graphic
communication, interiors and interactive design. We work in
partnership with both local and global brands on large and
small-scale projects. 'Creative knowledge' best describes
our offer, as within our unique, purpose-built studios, we
have both the raw talent and inventive thinkers to design in
every discipline – along with the experience, knowledge and
understanding to physically deliver.

Expertise
Retail & Interiors
Graphics & Point of Sale
Brand & Corporate Identity
Packaging
Exhibitions
Web & Multimedia

Clients
Amtico
Bentley Motors
Boots
Design Council
George at ASDA
Hammonds
Henri-Lloyd
KFC
Kohler Mira
Levi Strauss®
Marks and Spencer
Minton
Principles
Ray-Ban
Rolls-Royce
Royal Doulton
Speedo
Thorntons
Vodafone

Awards
Design Agency of the Year 2003
Marketing Magazine

Retail Interiors Awards 2002
Best Small Shop Single Store - Cinch

ISP/VM&SD International Store Interior Design
Competition 2002
Cinch - Special Award for Merchandising Concept

Retail Week Award 2001
Store Design of the Year
Lunn Poly Holiday Superstore

DBA Design Effectiveness Award 2000
Retail & Leisure Category - Levi's® London Project

See also Interior, Retail and Event Design p. 176

bentley identity

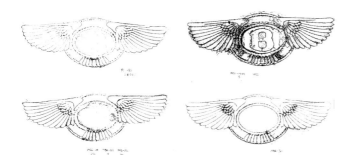

original car badge rubbings

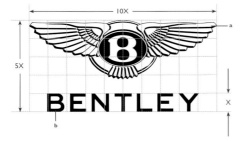

CREWE

GENUINE PARTS

crewe identity

ABCDEF B TUWYPV

bespoke typography

Design Bridge
Corporate and Service
Branding

18 Clerkenwell Close / London EC1R 0QN
T +44 (0)20 7814 9922 / F +44 (0)20 7814 9024
enquiries@designbridge.com
www.designbridge.com

Singapore Office / 5 Kadayanallur Street
Singapore 069183 / Singapore
T +65 6224 2336 / F +65 6224 2386
enquiries@designbridge.com
www.designbridge.com

Amsterdam Office / Keizersgracht 424
1016 GC Amsterdam / The Netherlands
T +31 (0)20 520 6030 / F +31 (0)20 520 6059
enquiries@designbridge.com
www.designbridge.com

Management Sir William Goodenough bt., Sophie Seveno
Contact Sophie Seveno
Staff 6 **Founded** 2000

At Design Bridge we believe brands are like people. They
come in all shapes and sizes, from the well-adjusted to
those with more deep-rooted problems and still more
waiting to be born. Whatever the scenario, we speak their
language and understand their needs. The common thread
is always fresh thinking, with every brief a new challenge.

Our particular strategic and creative skills can be used
individually, or in combination, to unlock the potential in
every brand. Whether the most compelling need for a new
corporate brand identity, promotional literature or a three-
dimensional expression of a brand, bespoke bottle or
graphic packaging, or even a digital media campaign, we
have over 15 years' experience helping companies around
the world to realise their goals, and those of their product
or service brands.

How do you communicate the personality and culture of
a business or organisation? How do you make sure your
customers understand the services you offer when there
is no tangible product? How can you get your message
heard in a sea of branded communication? We have
resolved those issues for many clients – both B2C and B2B.

See also Packaging Design p. 116

1   Thorogood, experts in business intelligence systems,
    supported a more focused positioning with a new
    corporate identity based on data cube expressed in
    script to underline their consultancy offering.
2   A strong and consistent brand language designed to
    complement the existing crest has given Everton Football
    Club an appropriate platform to communicate as a true
    Premier League club.
3   Building on the existing TNT brand equities but
    enhancing the brand palette to better communicate the
    values of TNT Logistics has helped support overall TNT
    brand awareness and perceptions in all markets.
4   The new 'smile' identity of the Norwegian food group
    Rieber & Son reflects the company's informal style and
    helps to communicate its core values of quality,
    approachability and food enjoyment.
5   Corporate sponsorship in the charitable sector is
    powerful in terms of building goodwill and reputation.
    Walk the World, a global employee fund-raising event
    organised by TPG was designed to raise awareness
    of world hunger and promote the activities of the UN
    World Food Programme. (see next page)

THOROGOOD
Get the full picture

1

2

3

insightful, confident, inspirational...

DESIGN BRIDGE

involved,
committed,
in touch...

Enterprise IG
The Global Brand Design Agency

11-33 St John Street / London EC1M 4PJ
T +44 (0)20 7559 7000 / F +44 (0)20 7559 7001
enquiries@enterpriseig.com
www.enterpriseig.co.uk

Contact Ms Robin Kadrnka, Group Marketing Director
Founded 1976

We've been around for over 25 years and are the world's leading global brand design agency, employing some 650 people in 24 offices worldwide. Part of the WPP Group, Enterprise IG works with leaders from most of the Fortune 500 companies to understand the challenges of the future and build brands that will succeed in constantly changing marketplaces.

We are passionate about helping companies to maximise the value of their intangible assets by building or evolving brands that are both compelling and true. We believe that successful branding needs to engage external audiences as well as internal audiences and our expertise in business and brand engagement ensures this balance.

Our challenge is to build brands that deliver on their core promises consistently across all dimensions and all media. Brands that are founded in what is compelling and true will outperform their competitors and sustain all stakeholders.

We've delivered business growth through successful corporate branding programmes for clients such as Vodafone, Merrill Lynch, BP, Deloitte, Shell, British Gas, SEAT, American Express, BBVA, Coca-Cola, TNT, Egg and ABN-AMRO.

See also Packaging Design p. 120 and Interior, Retail and Event Design p. 182

1 Deloitte, 2003
2 SAB Miller, 2003
3 Ministry of Sound, 2003
4 British Gas, 2003

38

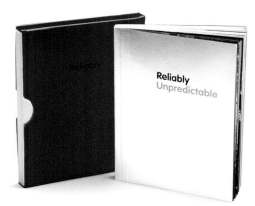

3

4

Fluid
Visual Communicators

1/222 The Custard Factory / Gibb Street
Birmingham B9 4AA
T +44 (0)121 693 6913 / F +44 (0)121 693 6911
drop@fluidesign.co.uk
www.fluidesign.co.uk

Management James Glover, Neil Roddis
Contact James Glover, james@fluidesign.co.uk
Founded 1995

Company Profile
Advertising/Branding/Design/Exhibition/Multimedia/
Packaging/Web

From brand identity to ad campaigns; from 3D modelling to
exhibitions; from packaging to web design – Fluid combine
a strategic approach with progressive design to provide
a solution that will fulfil all your requirements. Whether you
need a universal vision or unique attitude to an individual
project, Fluid's comprehensive knowledge and experience
ensure successful solutions on every level.

Clients Include
Adidas - Pursuit Marketing
BBC Worldwide
Birmingham Screen Festival
Camden Council
Capcom Europe
Coca-Cola
Electronic Arts
EMI Records
Fierce Earth
Infogrames
Levi's - Slice PR
Microsoft Xbox
Nivea/Beiersdorf
Nokia - Slice PR
Parlophone
Sony Computer Entertainment Europe
Sony Music Japan
T-26 Digital Type Foundry
Tesco
Ubi Soft
UK Film Council

1　Devil May Cry 2, Capcom Europe, 2003
2　Feed - Digital Expo, Fierce Earth, 2004
3　Ghosthunter, Sony Computer Entertainment, 2003
4　Rise to Honour, Sony Computer Entertainment, 2003
5　Fierce Festival, Fierce Earth, 2004
6　Nivea Body, Nivea/Beiersdorf, 2003
7　Bentley Rhythm Ace, Parlophone Records, 1999
8　Resident Evil: Dead Aim, Capcom Europe, 2003
9　Twisted Jeans Touring Stand, Levi's - Slice PR, 2001
10　Camden Design Awards, Camden Council, 2003
11　Burnout3: Takedown, Electronic Arts, Coming Soon

Fluid
British Design 2004/05
Branding, Graphic, Packaging & New Media Design
URBAN REGENERATION. VISUAL COMMUNICATION
BIRMINGHAM, UK

01 / Capcom Europe

Acfest
www.acfest.org

Infogrames
Xbox Games Promo CD/DVD

Screen West Midlands
www.screenwm.co.uk

Feed - Digital Expo
www.feedme.org.uk

Nuphonic
See www.fluidesign.co.uk

Sony Computer Entertainment
Christmas E-Card

Fierce Earth
www.fierce.info

PlayStation Europe
See www.fluidesign.co.uk

WORK EXAMPLES:

02 / Feed Festival

03 / Sony Computer Entertainment

04 / Sony Computer Entertainment

05 / Fierce Earth

06 / Nivea/Beiersdorf

07 / EMI Records

08 / Capcom Europe

09 / Levi's - Slice PR

10 / Camden Council

11 / Electronic Arts

Front Page Design

26 Woodside Place / Glasgow G3 7QL
T +44 (0)141 333 1808 / F +44 (0)141 333 1909
jackie@frontpage.co.uk
www.frontpage.co.uk

Management Ian McMillan & Felicity Johnson
Contact Jackie Arnott-Raymond
Staff 12 **Founded** 1990 **Membership** Design Business
Association

About Us

Established in 1990, Front Page is an award-winning graphic
design agency specialising in design for print, corporate
identity and digital media. Our talented team works hand in
hand with you, the client, to guarantee the successful
delivery of your project. Developing effective design
solutions that meet the needs of our clients is our priority,
and in a world of visual clutter we aim to communicate your
message with clarity and impact. All this and we're jolly nice
people to boot.

Clients

The Department for International Development
The Dialog Group
The Edinburgh Festival Fringe
The Edinburgh International Festival
Keith Prowse Attractions
The Robertson Group
The Royal Bank of Scotland
The Scottish Waste Awareness Group
Silverstone Motorsport Ltd
Simply Travel
The Walt Disney Company

1　The Simply Travel Group website
2　Walt Disney Parks & Resorts Travel Trade breakfast
　　promo pack
3　Silverstone Motorsport Annual Suite Hire direct mail
4　Edinburgh Festival Fringe Corporate Identity

1

2

3

4

Gensler
Studio 585

Roman House / Wood Street / London EC2Y 5BA
T +44 (0)20 7330 9600 / F +44 (0)20 7330 9630
info@gensler.com
www.gensler.com

Gensler – Studio 585
Studio 585 is the brand strategy graphic design resource at Gensler.

At 585 we believe great brands use words, images, products, environments, and services to create and maintain strong connections with their customers, employees, and the communities they serve.

We work with our clients to articulate their vision for the future and develop a brand strategy that embodies their identity, culture, experiences and aspirations.

As well as creating all the traditional materials related to a business-to-business or business-to-consumer brand, we are especially skilled at translating brand strategies into physical environmentsó whether they're corporate workplaces, resort hotels, showrooms, retail or other unique spaces – creating a compelling, recognizable experience.

The London Stock Exchange
Gensler worked with the London Stock Exchange to articulate a workspace brief, which communicates and supports their business objectives for the 21st century. This culminated in their move to Paternoster Square in May 2004. Gensler assisted with building consultation, interior design, graphic design, and wayfinding and signage services.

The branding and signage elements support the London Stock Exchange's brand style principles in an engaging environment, which enthuses staff and visitors about the capabilities and potential of this modern financial institution.

CAFE GRAPHICS & MERCHANDISE

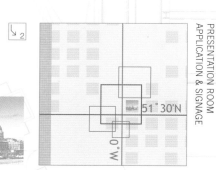

PRESENTATION ROOM APPLICATION & SIGNAGE

51° 30'N

0.0°W

London
STOCK EXCHANGE

3 BUILDING SIGNAGE
   & WAYFINDING PROTOCOL

4 RECEPTION AREA USING
   BESPOKE MATERIALS

5 MEETING ROOM
   CONCEPT & APPLICATION

6 INTERACTIVE WALL
   IN BREAKOUT AREAS

Hemisphere Design & Marketing Consultants

Binks Building / 30-32 Thomas Street / Northern Quarter
Manchester M4 1ER
T +44 (0)161 907 3730 / F +44 (0)161 907 3731
post@hemispheredmc.com
www.hemispheredmc.com

Management Sue Vanden, Grant Windridge
Contacts Sue Vanden, Grant Windridge
Staff 8 **Founded** 1988 **Membership** New York Type
Directors Club

Company Profile

"If a thing's worth doing, it's worth doing well" – an old adage maybe, but one that underpins everything we do.

Hemisphere's commitment to 'doing the right thing' applies to every aspect of our work – from the integrity of the design and marketing solutions we create to the way we treat our staff and customers, as well as our ongoing consideration of the impact we have on our environment.

With over sixteen years of experience, we devise intelligent, creative and strategic solutions to branding, promotional and communication challenges, all of them developed by combining quality of thought with quality of execution. Our projects range in scope from strategic branding consultancy through design for print and web to exhibition and environmental design, each discipline receiving the craft, ingenuity and attention to detail that are the hallmarks of Hemisphere's work.

Our ability to deliver on complex and wide-reaching identity issues has led to a number of high profile projects in place marketing and branding.

Clients

The Bridgewater Hall
Partners in Salford
Sunderland City Council
Northwest Development Agency
Manchester City Council
Marketing Manchester
Imperial War Museum North
Manchester Art Gallery
Royal Exchange Theatre
Metier Property Development
Sustainability Northwest
The Forestry Commission
Solar Century
United Co-operatives
Groundwork UK
Mersey Basin Campaign
Europride

1 Lime Sq. apartments marketing campaign, Metier
   Property Development
2 Brand implementation examples for the city of Salford
3 Industrial Evolution magazine, Sustainability
   Northwest/Northwest Development Agency
4 Identity and season print, The Bridgewater Hall
5 Manchester brand, font and Europride event identity

THE **bridgewater** HALL

46

2

3

5

Indigo Partnership
International
Brand Architects

35a Laitwood Road / London SW12 9QN / Balham
T +44 (0)208 772 0185 / T +44 (0)7801 688 957
F +44 (0)208 772 0561
kevin@indigopartners.co.uk
www.indigopartners.co.uk

Management Kevin McGurk, Sarah Kellaghan, Bob Grierson
Contact Kevin McGurk
Staff 10 **Founded** 1998

Realising Brand Potential

Behind every 'champion' is a dedicated team of professionals whose experience and objective advice builds on the competitor's unique strengths, minimises their weaknesses, constantly honing their skills to create a competitive edge.

We believe developing brands to become winners is no less challenging.

Successful brands don't just happen, they are driven by a determination to fulfil a potential opportunity not yet realised.

Indigo Partnership International has thirty years of experience developing successful brand strategies for our clients. We work in a discreet and collaborative way to bring objective insights that deliver real competitive advantage.

Our aim is to help you achieve your business objectives through consistent brand performance, market share growth and improved bottom-line profitability.

Effective branding is about winning, not just participating.

Clients
Bocts Healthcare International
B&Q – Planet Diamond Tools
Ferrero – Tic Tac
Mac Baren Pipe Tobacco
Marks & Spencer
Masterfoods – Whiskas
Pågen Bakery
Swedish Match – Borkum Riff,
Vin & Sprit – Absolut

See also Packaging Design p. 124

1   Tic Tac, The Ferrero Group
2   Pågen, Pågen Bakery
3   Snus, Swedish Match
4   Eryant & May, Swedish Match
5   Gothiatek, Swedish Match
6   Borkum Riff, Pipe Tobacco, Swedish Match

General

Infinite Design

56 Leazes Park Road / Newcastle upon Tyne NE1 4PG
T +44 (0)191 261 1160 / F +44 (0)191 261 2111
enquiries@infinitedesign.com
www.infinitedesign.com

Management Des Kennedy, Graham Morgan
Contacts Des Kennedy, Mel Whewell
Staff 8 **Founded** 1986

Company Profile

Infinite Design deliver creative, effective solutions in print, exhibition and digital media. We listen, think, consider and create every project with the intended audience in mind. We build strong relationships with our clients and work with them to achieve their objectives.

Clients

DanceCity
English Nature
Newcastle College
NHS Logistics
Northern Film & Media
Northumberland County Council
Orla Protein Technologies
Papworth Hospital NHS Trust
Saia Burgess
The British Museum
The National Trust
The Places for People Group
University of Newcastle upon Tyne
University of Plymouth

1 Infinite Design
2 Papworth Hospital NHS Trust, Annual Report
3 The National Trust, Wordsworth House Visitor Guides
4 Northern Film & Media, identity
5 The Places for People Group, Annual Report
6 Greyscale, product catalogues
7 Dancexchange, classes literature

1

2

3

5

NORTHERN
FILM+MEDIA
PEOPLE

NORTHERN
FILM+MEDIA
COMPANIES

NORTHERN
FILM+MEDIA
AUDIENCES

NORTHERN
FILM+MEDIA
IDEAS

4

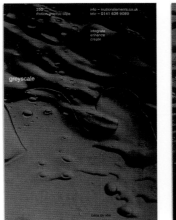

6

7

Kiwi
Creative solutions for all media

96 Broad Street / Birmingham B15 1AU
T +44 (0)121 688 8881
birmingham@kiwi.co.uk
www.kiwi.co.uk

2 Millharbour / Docklands / London E14 9TE
T +44 (0)20 7750 9940
london@kiwi.co.uk
www.kiwi.co.uk

Contacts John White, Terri Smart
Staff 14 **Founded** 1996

Our purpose is simple: helping all our clients, some very
large, others relatively small, the seriously global and the
necessarily local, commercial and public, to communicate
effectively.

We produce work for all media. It is driven by an
understanding of clients' real needs and pays close
attention to detail as well as the big picture.

Above all, we bring real creativity to bear across the
spectrum, drawing on the complementary mix of
experience, skills and talents represented by our designers,
writers and planners, to bring powerful dynamics to
communications.

We do not believe that the devil should have all the
best tunes. We do not agree that only the big battalions
should win.

We believe that all our clients, large and small, should
always win. When they win, so do we. And that is how it
should be.

See also New Media Design p. 156

'curiosity is the key to creativity'
Akio Morita (1921 -)
www.kiwi.co.uk/curious

Lloyd Northover
Vivid brands, clear communications

2 Goodge Street / London W1T 2QA
T +44 (0)20 7420 4850 / F +44 (0)20 7420 4858
neil.hudspeth@lloydnorthover.com
www.lloydnorthover.com

Contacts Jim Northover, Neil Hudspeth
Founded 1975 **Memberships** DBA, D&AD, CSD, BDI

Company Profile

Lloyd Northover is a team of bright, inventive, down-to-earth people devoted to creating vivid brands and clear communications – across traditional and digital media, in two dimensions and three. At the heart of the company is our belief that design has the power to make a real difference to business and society, and to produce tangible returns on money spent. It's what we call creative value.

On our team we have designers, consultants, researchers, copywriters, architects, web developers and project managers who think and work together to come up with inventive answers to strategic problems. From brief to delivery, we draw on our clients' insights as well as our own for richer results.

Our services include brand strategy and corporate identity; interactive media and e-marketing; stakeholder, internal and marketing communications; literature; information design; and environments. As part of a bigger family, Incepta Group plc, we can also give our clients access to specialised talent in public relations, advertising, marketing services and research.

If you like what you see here, do get in touch and we'll tell you more about what we've done, who we've done it for and how we can do it for you.

Clients

Allied Irish Bank
Bank of America Capital Partners Europe
Barbican
British Council
China Light & Power (Hong Kong)
Christian Salvesen
Continental Airlines
Doughty Hanson
Freeserve
GlaxoSmithKline
Health Protection Agency
Home Office
Invesco Perpetual
John Lewis Partnership
KCR Corporation (Hong Kong)
Land Transport Authority (Singapore)
Manchester Airport
Messer Group (Germany)
Millennium Hotels (Singapore)
Nasdaq
National Savings and Investments
Taylor Woodrow
University of Manchester
Welsh Development Agency
Xstrata (Switzerland)

See also New Media Design p. 158

Queen's University Belfast

barbican

leapfrog

to Manchester Airport

Lloyd Northover

The Staffordshire

national savings
& investments

ns&i

issue ▶ 01   expires
end ▶ 03/08
J WILSON
Account number ▶ 123456789

633625981234567890

OI
zero one

© GwirFlas
TrueTaste
Cymru y
Wales the

Events | Recipes | Producers | Press releases | Pu

**Welsh food and drink.
A secret worth sharing.**

Select an option
→ Home
→ Links
→ Feedback

Wales prides itself on supplying some of the fine
produce in the world. This new site will help you
the most of Welsh food and drink.
On this site you'll find lots of information about W
food: everything from recipes to local food fairs a
producer listings.
Over the coming months, you will see many mor
exciting features added to the site - don't forget
come back.

Loines Furnival
Design and Communications Consultants

9 Abbey Square / Chester CH1 2HU
T +44 (0)1244 310 456 / F +44 (0)1244 311 044
sara.sartorius@l-f.co.uk
www.loines-furnival.co.uk

Management Mike Loines, John Furnival
Contact Sara Sartorius, New Business Manager,
sara.sartorius@l-f.co.uk
Staff 15 **Founded** 1982
Membership Design Business Association

Company Profile
Loines Furnival offer a winning combination of an innovative
and strategic approach to communications, coupled with
creative design excellence.

Founded in 1982 by managing partners Mike Loines and
John Furnival, our mission is 'to produce outstanding,
award-winning design and communications solutions
tailored to the strategic needs of our clients'.

We offer the following services:
Strategic communications planning and implementation
Branding/corporate identity design and implementation
Design for print
Design and building of internet/intranet sites
Corporate responsibility reporting
Signing and vehicle livery design and implementation
Design for advertising

Clients
Camelot Group PLC
Centrica
United Utilities
Powergen
The University of Liverpool
EDF Energy
Wates Group
North West Development Agency

The University of Liverpool
annual report

The University of Liverpool
corporate and marketing literature

Amey plc
corporate responsibility report

56

Camelot Group plc
web and print reporting

United Utilities plc
corporate and customer communications

England's Northwest
brand development

Northwest Development Agency
corporate literature and advertising

Lattice Group plc
corporate responsibility report

Lunartik

Studio 4 / 9 Carisbrooke Rd / Birmingham B17 8NN
T +44 (0)7967 803 909
matt@lunartik.com
www.lunartik.com

Contact Matt Jones
Founded 2002

Company Profile
At Lunartik, a love of tea has fuelled some 6 years of graphic
and product design shenanigans. Work that's spanned
everything from funky consumer goods, websites and
illustrations to limited edition designer toys.

We're as comfortable working digitally as we are with pen
and ink. And if the deadline calls for it, or we're just into what
we're doing, we're more than happy to work under the cover
of darkness. It's all part of a commitment to treat our clients
as people, rather than just pay cheques.

To find out what we could do for you and why there's art
at the heart of lunartik, visit us at www.lunartik.com

Services Include
Product design & development
Design consultancy
Illustration
Stickers
Website design
Web graphics & animation
Copywriting

Clients
TOY2R
Playlounge
Hana TimePiece Company
Artsnose Ltd
Guinea pig design
Zucco ltd
Pictoplasma
NookArt Pty Ltd

Web Links
un-plugged.co.uk
artsnose.com
blaineinthebox.com
nockart.com
ascotoem.com

www.lunartik.com

58

Minx Creative
www.minxcreative.com

2 Old Library Court / 45 Gillender Street / London E14 6RN
T +44 (0)20 7510 1005 / F +44 (0)20 7510 1007
team@minxcreative.com
www.minxcreative.com

Management Roz Nazerian, Nicola Denton
Staff 4 **Founded** 1997 **Membership** British Design Initiative

Company Profile
Minx Creative is an independent, multi-disciplinary creative consultancy specialising in all areas of graphics for print, multimedia, display and web design.

For further information please visit our website or contact us direct.

Clients
ACL
Alcatel Telecom
Asian Women's Resource Centre
British Maritime Technology
Centre for British Teachers
Connexions
ColourNation
Cup Group
Cytec Solutions
Department for Education and Skills
JCDecaux
Liss Systems
Lombard Odier Darier Hentsch
London Borough of Brent
London Borough of Camden
London Borough of Southwark
London Borough of Tower Hamlets
London West IAG Partnership
Marine Science and Technology
Oxfordshire IAG
Race on the Agenda
Republic PR
Royal Pharmaceutical Society
Sure Start
United Biscuits

1   Lovefootball logo generation, Cup Group, 2003
2   Borough-wide service literature, London Borough of Camden / Sure Start, 2004
3   21st anniversary poster campaign, Asian Women's Resource Centre, 2003
4   Corporate identity programme, Liss Systems, 2004
5   Screen presentation branding, Lombard Odier Darier Hentsch, 2003
6   Careers service literature, Centre for British Teachers / Connexions, 2004
7   Exhibition graphics, Alcatel Telecom, 2003
8   Corporate identity programme, ColourNation, 2004
9   'Agenda' quarterly journal, Race on the Agenda, 2004
10 Arts and events literature, London Borough of Tower Hamlets, 2004
11 Arts and events logo generation, London Borough of Tower Hamlets, 2003

60

1

2

3

4

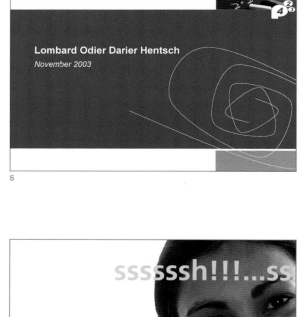

5

6

7

8

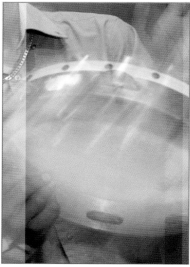

9

10

11

Navyblue Design Group

122 Giles Street / Edinburgh EH6 6BZ
T +44 (0)131 553 5050 / F +44 (0)131 555 0707
edinburgh@navyblue.com
www.navyblue.com

Third Floor Morelands / 17-21 Old Street
London EC1V 9HL
T +44 (0)20 7253 0316 / F +44 (0)20 7553 9409
london@navyblue.com
www.navyblue.com

Management Douglas Alexander, Managing Director
Navyblue Scotland, Geoff Nicol, Managing Director
Navyblue London
Contacts Mike Lynch, Business Development Director,
Toby Southgate, Client Services Director
Staff 68 **Founded** 1994

Company Profile
Navyblue's core business is creative design and
communications, supported by internal strategic planning
and research – one of our values is "thinking out louder™",
and this approach influences everything we do. Since 1994
we have expanded our skill-set from traditional graphics into
the areas of 3d environments and new media, incorporating
technical development expertise as well as on-screen
design capability. Navyblue is one of the UK's top 30 design
consultancies, employing more than 65 people and with
a turnover in excess of £7 million.

Graphics and Branding
The huge scope of graphics and branding work is truly
reflected in the diversity of our clients and our credentials.
We work across the whole spectrum of industry sectors
on projects ranging from Annual Reports, through new
product launches and promotions, to brand refreshes and
full re-branding exercises. Our cross-disciplined capability
allows clients to gain significant value and generate
economies of scale by thinking up front, then delivering
through the most appropriate creative medium.

Clients
Bright Grey – identity creation, branding, literature design,
consumer website design and build, IFA extranet design
and build, internal signage and environments, ongoing
communications
Ellesse – brand awareness materials, seasonal catalogues,
point-of-sale brand expression
GF Smith – promotional literature, UK product launch
Glanbia plc – annual report & accounts
Hilton Group plc – annual report & accounts
Jack Morton Worldwide – promotional literature, 2002
Commonwealth Games, Manchester
Learning Skills Council – annual report & accounts
Newcastle International – rebranding exercise, identity
creation, brand guidelines, internal and external signage
Robert Horne – promotional literature
Scottish & Newcastle plc – annual report & accounts

**See also Packaging Design p. 130, New Media Design
p. 160 and Interior, Retail and Event Design p. 194**

1 Bright Grey brand creation and communications material
2 Newcastle International Airport brand creation
3 Jack Morton International, Manchester Commonwealth
  Games 2002 commemorative book
4 Robert Horne/Fulmar/Navyblue promotional material

bright grey™

1

4

Newcastle International

Studio North

6 Bradley Street / Northern Quarter / Manchester M1 1EH
T +44 (0)161 237 5151 / F +44 (0)161 237 5131
creativity@studionorth.co.uk
www.studionorth.co.uk

Contacts Dan Hulse, Nick Wright, Michael Di Paola
Staff 7 **Founded** 2001

Company Profile
If the world is now a global village, then the brand is the
language in which it communicates. Here at Studio North,
we're committed to ensuring that every brand we develop
speaks to its audience in an emotive, truthful and alluring
dialect. Raising awareness is just the beginning of the
process – we go much, much further.

Our commitment to routing out your core selling proposition
is clear. You'll spot it in the questions we ask...
Who are you talking to?
What are you saying to them?
Why should they believe you?
We'll get to the bottom of your marketing issues and
provide you with solutions that not only reach, but excite
and convince your potential audience.

Turning your requirements into creative concepts and
high quality presentation materials is not just something
we're good at. It's what we thrive on. And the reason
we're experiencing fast and continuous growth in such a
competitive and saturated market.

Fresh Ideas. Creative Energy. Intelligent Strategy.

Head North.

Clients
BP Oil
British Waterways
Co-operative Group
Dixons Group
DTE Group
Dunlop Heywood Lorenz
Genesis Communications
Green Isle Foods
ICI-Dulux
Imagine Recruitment
Knowsley Council
Manchester Chamber of Commerce
Manchester City Council
NHS
Readymix
Serco
Stagecoach
Syncro
Tesco
Total (UK)
Total Fitness
Trafford Community Leisure Trust
Tyco
UMIST

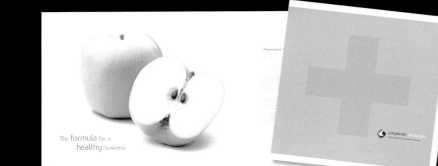

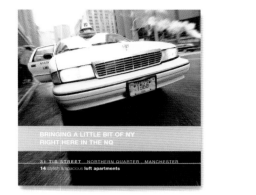

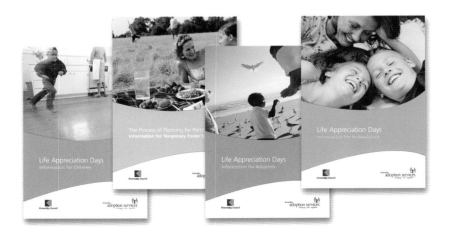

Odd
Design Led Creative Agency

5th Floor / 159-173 St. John Street / London EC1V 4QJ
T –44 (0)20 7663 1790 / F +44 (0)20 7336 8789
believe@thankodd.com
www.thankodd.com

Management Simon Glover, Nick Stickland
Contacts Simon Glover, Nick Stickland
Staff 8 **Founded** 2001

What is Odd?
Odd is a design-led creative agency offering bespoke
solutions that enable consumers to interact with brands
in new and exciting ways.

We liberate consumers from traditional advertising
mediums and communication methods using Brand
Physicality to create more engaging experiences.
Using creative, tangible media and three-dimensional
environments, Brand Physicality communicates on
an experiential level and cuts through by reaching
consumers at key points in their day-to-day lives.

The team at Odd draws on experience from many
disciplines: architecture, advertising, online, product
and graphic design.

Clients
Abbey
BBC Radio 4
Blueprint Magazine
De-construct
Elvis
Grey London
Heineken
Honda
Hypertelic Records
Karmarama
Kerrang 105.2
Kiss FM
Lime
Naked Communications
Sen Health
Siemens Xelibri
Sony PlayStation 2

Oliis Design
Brand Design and Strategy

14a-16a The Arches / Goswell Hill / Windsor
Berkshire SL4 1RH
T +44 (0)1753 857 575 / F +44 (0)1753 857 171
info@oliisdesign.com
www.oliisdesign.com

Management Natalie Spearing
Contacts Natalie Spearing, Himalee Rupesinghe
Founded 1997

Intelligent Marketing, Pure Design
Oliis is a multi-disciplined design and marketing agency.
We create, manage and support your creative vision by
providing dynamic and intelligent design, technology and
marketing solutions that address each client's commercial
needs.

Our strength is shown in our ability to translate your vision
across a number of mediums, providing inspirational and
innovative solutions that really work.

Clients include
Charter UK
Chester Boyd
Coca-Cola Enterprises Limited
Co-operative Funeralcare
Cosworth Technology
CPM International
DeLaRue Interclear
Experior
Freeads.co.uk
Gaggenau
Goodyear Dunlop
InterContinental Hotels Group
Nissan Europe
O2
Onyx Software
Optometry Giving Sight
VNU Publications

1   Nissan, Brand Management
2   O2, Retail Strategy
3   OGS, Global Brand & Marketing Campaign
4   CPM, Visual Identity Programme
5   Gaggenau, Advertising & Internal Communications

70

1

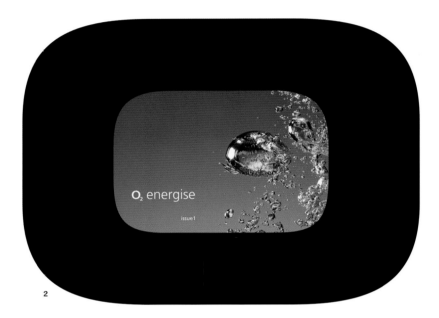

O₂ energise

issue 1

2

Y
O U
CAN HELP
US TO GIVE
OTHERS SIGHT

JOIN US IN HELPING TO ELIMINATE THE MAIN
CAUSES OF AVOIDABLE BLINDNESS AND IMPAIRED
VISION AROUND THE WORLD – TOGETHER WE CAN
ENABLE PEOPLE TO EXERCISE THEIR RIGHT TO SIGHT

OPTOMETRY**GIVINGSIGHT**

3

4

5

oliis^d

Oliis' ability to think laterally and provide both strategic and creative responses is a real asset to our business. They have played a vital role, and still continue to support our global identity programme and share our vision for the future of the brand. We are proud of our partnership with Oliis.
Stephanie Gonier, Nissan Europe

Oliis' complete understanding of our business enabled them to create and implement our new visual identity across all mediums, whilst fulfilling the business' needs, hence achieving a solution which far exceeded our expectations.
Martin Ryan, CPM International

Oliis deliver. They appreciate what we need and create imaginative, functional solutions. The depth of their understanding of our brand is impressive. Their project management passionate.
Philip Winter, Gaggenau

Oliis' strategic and creative thinking, and their ability to understand different audiences have meant that our staff training will now be based on the materials they developed for us. We are always delighted with their enthusiasm and hands on approach to each project.
Becky Hughes, O2

OPX
Visual Communication and Brand Strategy

51 Hoxton Square / London N1 6PB
T +44 (0)20 7729 6295 / F +44 (0)20 7729 8837
postbox@opx.co.uk
www.opx.co.uk

Management William Bickerstaff, Simon Goodall, Antony Harrington, Frances Jackson
Contacts Simon Goodall, Frances Jackson
Staff 8 **Founded** 1992 **Memberships** D&AD, DBA, STD

Specialisms
Brand strategy
Visual identity systems
Website design

Approach
OPX are a committed and experienced team leading change through design. Each project, poster to website, or annual report to visual identity, is unique. We work with our clients to identify and understand the challenges they face, working in partnership to produce effective work of beauty and impact.

Recent Clients
AECOM
BAE Systems
BRE
ERM
FaberMaunsell
Higrade
Hochtief
Scott Brownrigg
RIBA
RPA

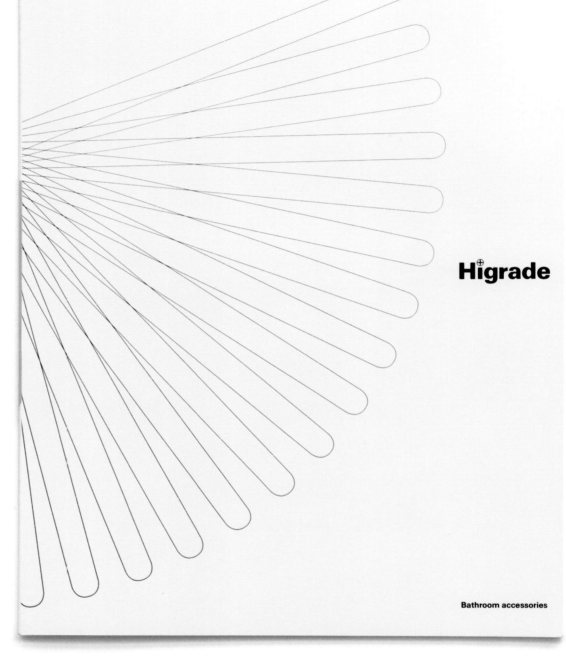

Higrade

Bathroom accessories

SCOTT BROWNRIGG

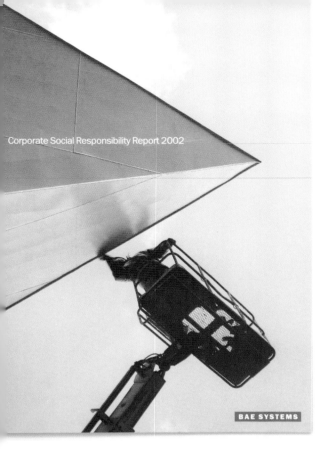

Corporate Social Responsibility Report 2002

BAE SYSTEMS

BRE

new housing from old buildings

constructing the future

Working with the community
Quality management
New life test methods

Parkmount Housing
Richard Partington Architects

FABER MAUNSELL
Annual Review 2003

Thinking about tomorrow...

R Design

Studio 3, Church Studios / Camden Park Road
London NW1 9AY
T +44 (0)20 7284 5840 / F +44 (0)20 7284 5849
dave@r-email.co.uk
www.r-website.co.uk

Management David Richmond
Staff 5 **Founded** 1990

Company Profile
R Design offers straightforward, simple, creative solutions
that meet the brief. If you want a straight-talking creative,
simply come and meet us.

Clients
Boaters
Melon Maternity (Los Angeles)
Sel²ridges
Tesco
The Food Doctor
WH Smith
Woolworths

See also Packaging Design p. 138

Is your food good to you?

Food intolerance testing available
You may love food, but does your food love you?
Few people actually have allergies, but many can react badly
to the food they eat.

THE**FOODDOCTOR**™
A Recipe for Health & Vitality

www.thefooddoctor.com

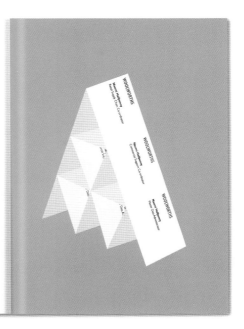

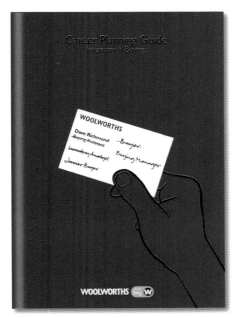

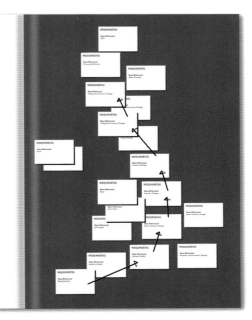

Red Cell Scotland

Thomson House / 8 Minerva Way / Glasgow G3 8AU
T +44 (0)141 221 6882 / F +44 (0)141 221 5763
simon_macquarrie@redcellnetwork.com
www.redcellglasgow.com

Management Simon MacQuarrie, Jonathan Frewin
Contacts Simon MacQuarrie, Jonathan Frewin
Staff 20 **Founded** 1974

Company Profile

Red Cell Scotland is a fully integrated creative marketing and communication agency, offering expertise in advertising, branding, design for print and new media, direct mail and strategic planning.

We are a member of WPP's Red Cell Network, a network which comprises over 50 offices in Europe, North America and Asia.

We place great emphasis on actively fostering creative thinking, nurturing talent and supporting our creative skills with strong client service and project management teams. These teams form the backbone of the agency. They provide the practical skills, in-depth knowledge, understanding and experience in progressing creative work smoothly and efficiently from concept to project completion. Working together with the creative department, these teams ensure that, at all levels, all of our clients receive optimum service and obtain the greatest possible value from our broad skill base.

1   Scotland the Brand, brand identity
2   Skye, the Island and Lochalsh, brand identity and application
3   Glasgow International Piping Festival, brand name, identity and application
4   Tullibardine Retail / Visitor attraction, brand identity and application
5   CALA Homes, Glasgow Harbour brand identity and application
6   CALA Homes, Eclipse brand identity and application

1

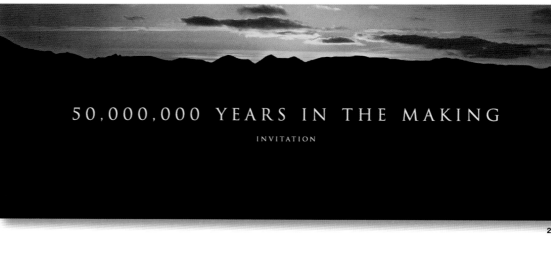

50,000,000 YEARS IN THE MAKING
INVITATION

2

Tullibardine
The Essence of Scotland

3   4

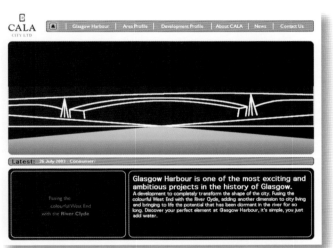

JUST ADD WATER

FIND YOUR IDEAL ENVIRONMENT AT GLASGOW HARBOUR

CALA'S NEW LUXURY WATERFRONT DEVELOPMENT

CALA
CITY LTD

URBAN SPACE REFRESHED

CALA
CITY LTD | Glasgow Harbour | Area Profile | Development Profile | About CALA | News | Contact Us

Latest: 26 July 2003 · Consumers queued for over 40 hours to reserve one of CALA's apartments

Area Profile
> Location
> Getting There
> Site Plan

Glasgow is not only Scotland's largest city it's also without a doubt its freshest and most innovative. An ancient heritage combines effortlessly with a youthful energy across everything from theatre and art to clubs, restaurants and bars. Glasgow has more acres of green space within its boundaries than any other city in Europe. It's the UK's second shopping city. Its universities, colleges and art schools are world class. It's home to some of Scotland's top independent schools. And it's alive and enjoying life to the full 24 hours a day, 7 days a week. Redefine urban living in the city that defined it in the first place.

Glasgow Harbour is one of the most exciting and ambitious projects in the history of Glasgow. A development to completely transform the shape of the city. Fusing the colourful West End with the River Clyde, adding another dimension to city living and bringing to life the potential that has been dormant in the river for so long. Discover your perfect element at Glasgow Harbour, it's simple, you just add water.

5

COULD YOU BE
THE FACE OF ECLIPSE?

www.calaeclipse.co.uk

ECLIPSE
ST MARY'S GATE
SHEFFIELD

CALA
HOMES

ECLIPSE
ST MARY'S GATE
SHEFFIELD

LUXURY STUDIO 1 & 2 BEDROOM APARTMENTS

CALA apartment enquiries Tel: 0113 239 9500
www.calaeclipse.co.uk

CALA
HOMES

Tel: 0113 239 9500
www.calaeclipse.co.uk

6

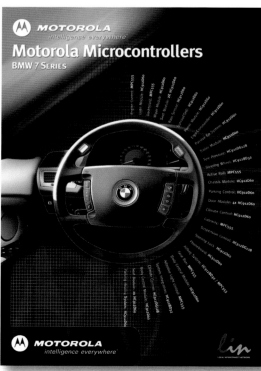

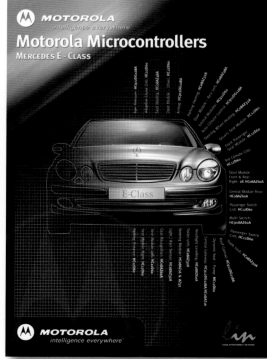

11

12

13

Spin

12 Canterbury Court / 1-3 Brixton Road / Kennington Park
London SW9 6DE
T +44 (0)20 7793 9555 / F +44 (0)20 7793 9666
patricia@spin.co.uk
www.spin.co.uk

Management Patricia Finegan, Tony Brook
Contact Patricia Finegan
Staff 11 **Founded** 1992 **Memberships** British Design & Art
Direction, Design Business Association

Company Profile
Established in 1992, Spin work across a variety of areas
including branding, print, retail, broadcast and moving
image. Spin's approach delivers clear communicative work
with strong concepts.

Clients
British Council
Caruso St John
Central Office of Information
Channel 4 Broadcasting
Christies
Deutsche Bank
Diesel
Five Broadcasting
Greater London Authority
Haunch of Venison
Health Education Authority
Ileana Makri
Levi Strauss & Co
MTV
Nike
Nokia
Orange
Photographer's Gallery
Precise Reprographics
Project 2
Rankin
Tate Modern
UBS
Vision-On Publishing
VH-1
Whitechapel Gallery

See also New Media Design p. 164

Springetts

13 Salisbury Place / London W1H 1FJ
T +44 (0)20 7486 7527 / F +44 (0)20 7487 3033
all@springetts.co.uk
www.springetts.co.uk

Management Andy Black, Roger Bannister
Contact Brendan Thorpe
Staff 41

Company Profile

As one of the UK's top independently owned branding and design consultancies, Springetts has a range of clients from small and local to big and global. Branding can take many forms: a new corporate identity for a major energy supplier, a new brand identity for a well-established fmcg product range or a complete overhaul for one of the world's largest football clubs. Springetts has the expertise and experience to offer branding solutions whatever the size and nature of the project.

See also Packaging Design p. 142

1 Manchester United: creation of a new identity system, signage, stationery, tickets, licensing, brand guidelines
2 Barclaycard: corporate identity, sub-brand identities, web site, signage
3 Dairy Crest: a revised and authoritative brand identity for Cathedral City
4 Powergen: corporate identity system, stationery, interior design, web site, Powerpoint, brand guidelines
5 Get Sorted!: corporate identity for a network of marketing consultants, stationery
6 Epsom Downs Racecourse: a new and distinctive identity system, individual race and event identities, signage
7 Rugby Football Union: creation of a new identity system, signage, licensing, stationery, brand guidelines

Springetts.co.uk

Brand Positioning

Naming

Brand & Corporate Identity

Structural Design

N.P.D

Licensing

ENGLAND
RUGBY®

Start Creative Limited

2 Sheraton Street / Soho / London W1F 8BH
T +44 (0)20 7269 0101 / F +44 (0)20 7269 0102
jen@startcreative.co.uk
startcreative.co.uk

Management Mike Curtis, Darren Whittingham,
Jennifer McAleer, Ian Kempen **Contact** Jennifer McAleer
Staff 59 **Founded** 1996

Company Profile
We're in the business of ideas and creativity. Here, we think
differently and this makes Start an exciting place to be.

Start is a creative agency with one aim – to deliver inspiring
creativity to meet business needs. We have burning passion
for three things – branding, marketing and digital media.
We specialise, we integrate and we deliver, using five sets
of skills – strategy, design, writing, production, and project
management.

We have enjoyed eight years of progressive growth. Now
we are the 10th largest independent creative agency in the
UK. Our clients include some of Britain's best brands. Last
year we won numerous effectiveness awards. We attract
and nurture some 60 of the industry's most talented people,
whose creative minds are dedicated to the needs of our
clients.

Clients
Virgin
BBC
Royal Mail
Hertz
Ordnance Survey
Interserve plc
Thetrainline
uSwitch
Land Registry
Nelsonbach
Transport for London
Department of Health
COI Communications
UK Trade & Investment
Fox Williams
Cisco Systems
Azzurri

**See also Packaging Design p. 144, New Media Design
p. 166 and Interior, Retail and Event Design p. 202**

1   Ordnance Survey Partner Programme
2   Virgin Mobile catalogue
3   Hertz Tour Operator CD Rom and brochure
4   Royal Mail poster campaign for Special Stamps
5   Royal Mail Special Stamps promotional mailing packs

1

NO STRINGS.
JUST GREAT PHONES, 3P TEXTS
AND ONE SIMPLE TARIFF.

TRUST
We don't need a piece of paper to stay together.

91% of our customers like us enough to recommend us

69% have already told their mates about us

71% of our customers are extremely or very satisfied

That's why we're the only UK mobile operator to have won both these awards for the third year running.

KEEP IT SIMPLE

Just 15p a minute
for the first 5 minutes of calls each day...

...and 5p a minute after that
for all standard UK calls and calls to other Virgin Mobile phones.

Pay the same – day or night
If you don't use your phone, you don't pay. And if you do, you do.

Call more to get back more
• Earn free airtime every month you spend over £30 on calls and texts made from the UK and to countries abroad.
• Connect a mate to save money on calls and texts with Glue.
• Pick up free airtime with Funshot.
For more details, see pages 6 and 7.

Voicemail costs you nothing
It's free to pick up your voicemail in the UK – perfect handy for retrieving business messages or if you're trying to avoid your latest drunken mishap.

Fair tariff to all networks
• 35p a minute for all calls to other UK networks.
• 10p to text all other UK networks.
For more details, turn over the page.

→ 0845 6000 600

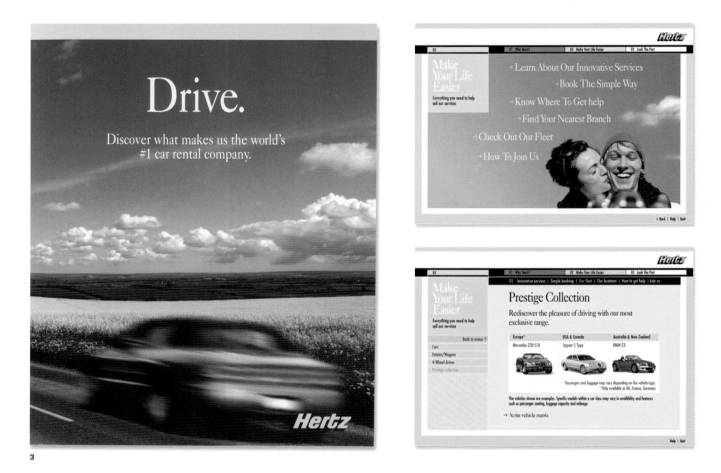

3

Glenelly Valley, Sperrins Northern Ireland

47

Just like the real thing, only smaller

Northern Ireland stamps: out 16 March

Available as Mint Stamps, First Day Covers*, Presentation Packs and Stamp Cards.

Glenfinnan Viaduct, Lochaber Scotland

47

Scotland at your fingertips

The beauty and colours of Scotland's landscapes are vividly brought to life by this set of six special stamps. Available from 15 July as Mint Stamps, Presentation Packs, First Day Covers (day of issue only), and Stamp Cards. Ask for them at your local Post Office® branch, call 0845 072 2000 or visit www.royalmail.com/stamps

All you need to know about stamps...

Presentation Packs

Stamp fact: The most popular issue of Special Stamps was the Victory set produced in 1946 – it sold an incredible 43 million.

"In 60 years of collecting, I've seen stamps from all over the world. My favourite has to be the commemorative stamp issued for the Festival of Britain. It's a simple design but for me the important thing is the strength of the memories it brings back."

Taxi Studio Ltd

93 Princess Victoria Street / Clifton / Bristol BS8 4DD
T +44 (0)117 973 5151 / F +44 (0)117 973 5181
alex@taxistudio.co.uk
www.taxistudio.co.uk

Management Spencer Buck, Alex Bane, Lorna Sturrock,
Ryan Wills **Contact** Alex Bane
Staff 7 **Founded** 2002 **Membership** DBA

Company Profile

Hello. Thanks for being interested enough by the pictures on
the right to read this bit on the left. So, what do you want to
know? Are we any good? We think so, but more importantly,
our clients think so too. They invest a lot of money with us,
and in return, we deliver original creative solutions that not
only answer the brief but also have a habit of picking up
awards along the way. Since our foundation on June 1st
2002, we've (drunkenly) received over 25 design awards and
one non-design award from Shell for the way we run our
business – still, we don't let any of that go to our heads.

Taxi Studio is a multi-disciplinary creative consultancy
fuelled by Big Ideas. Our job is to build brands, awareness,
friendships and (most importantly) sales. Whether you
require packaging, literature, point-of-sale, branding, name
generation or advertising (have I missed anything?), we'll
communicate your proposition to your target audience in
a unique and memorable way. If you'd like to know more
about us, please give Alex Bane a call at the studio on
+44 (0)117 973 5151, on his mobile +44 (0)7801 598 569
or via email: alex@taxistudio.co.uk

Clients

Clarks
Ravel
Somerfield
First Group
Integralis

1. Clarks required a strong idea for their local advertising.
   The posters had to inform customers about a new store
   opening in their area. Here's an idea on a shoestring
   budget that looks a million dollars.
2. Identity for the Clarks and Ravel sales team member's
   in-store incentive scheme.
3. This logo works because of the use of 'negative' space,
   perfect for Viewpoint Photography.
4. Clarks needed a name and brand identity for their new
   premium range of handbags and accessories. Toco is
   derived from 'tocco', Italian for 'touch'.
5. A heavyweight collaboration between Taxi Studio and
   the Clarks in-house design team.
6. To effectively communicate the freshness of Somerfield's
   new soups, we went back to the chalkboard.
7. Realising that dolly mixtures and strawberry laces etc.
   aren't solely the domain of children, we designed this
   sweet range with adults in mind too.

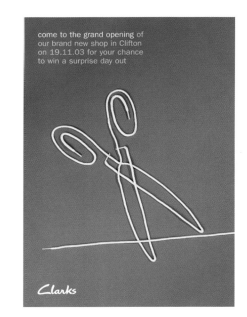

5

6

7

Two by Two
Design Consultants

348 Goswell Road / London EC1V 7LQ
T +44 (0)20 7278 1122 / F +44 (0)20 7278 1155
zebra@twobytwo.co.uk
www.twobytwo.co.uk

Management Salvatore Cicero, Ashwin Shaw
Contacts Salvatore Cicero, Ashwin Shaw
Staff 12 **Founded** 1995

Company Profile
Yadda yadda 1995 yadda yadda yadda yadda
yadda packaging, branding, interiors yadda yadda
yadda yadda yadda yah.

Originality breeds content

Clients include
Ccuture Brands
Dudley plc
Elemis London Ltd
Europa Office
Magnelli
L'Oreal
Richard Ward
Royal Mint
J Sainsbury plc
Satyajit Ray Foundation
Teenage Cancer Trust
The Wine Society
Verco

See also Packaging Design p. 146

1   Magnelli Italian Coffee Company

Word of
Visual Communication

50/52 Church St. Ashbourne / Derbyshire DE6 1AJ
T +44 (0)1335 348 288
info@wordof.uk.com
www.wordof.uk.com

Toyota's new corporate literature was created by a design consultancy that employs no designers...

No Art Directors
No Creative Directors
No Mac Operators
No Production Managers
No Copywriters
and, above all, No Account Handlers

Word of is a virtual company. Our clients talk directly to the people who do the work. And the people who do the work are members of a team of experienced Creative Associates that has taken fifteen years to assemble.

Major talent is never cheap but, when utilised and managed correctly, it can deliver outstanding value... as well as outstanding quality.

'Word of has been working with Toyota UK since 1992, the year we began operations in the East Midlands and North Wales. Working closely with us in an on-going partnership, they continue to demonstrate their skills in many areas and their multi-disciplined approach provides an ideal one stop shop' ...delivering total synergy and continuity.'

Doctor Bryan Jackson OBE, Managing Director
Toyota Motor Manufacturing (UK) Limited

Recent Awards
Winner Epson Creativity award New York 2003
Regional winner Robert Horne Group Shout awards 2003
Overall winner Robert Horne Group Shout awards 2003

Clients Include
adidas
Boots the Chemist
British Airways
Ciber UK
Coats Viyella
Dixons Stores Group
JCB
Menuez Pictures
Orange
Toyota
Waitrose

1   Toyota and the environment
2   Toyota and Europe
3   Toyota and the community
4   Christmas card
5   Christmas card
6   Tenth anniversary branding
7   Avensis UK/Japan export branding

1

2

3

a breath of fresh air

N_2 78.084% O_2 20.947% Ar 0.934% CO_2 0.033%

Toyota regards the protection of the global environment
as one of its top-priority concerns. At every stage of a vehicle's life,
Toyota strives to protect the environment through optimising energy
efficiency and reducing harmful wastage.

Toyota's commitment to the environment extends to all areas of its operations. In 1992, its Global Policy established action guidelines known as Toyota's 'Earth Charter' with three key objectives: First, to develop technologies that minimise the environmental impact of vehicles and their manufacture. Secondly, to evaluate and minimise the environmental impact at every stage of the product's life-cycle. Finally, to support and actively participate in a diverse range of global environmental protection activities. In 1999 Toyota became the first carmaker to win the United Nations Environment Programme Global 500 Award, an award given to companies that make outstanding contributions in the field of environmental protection. Toyota Manufacturing UK's environmental policy reflects Toyota's global earth charter. It was Toyota's first overseas plant and the UK's first car manufacturer to achieve ISO 14001 certification. It was also the first overseas Toyota plant to use water-borne paints. All Toyota's efforts are underpinned by its 5Rs philosophy that seeks to eliminate the amount of waste involved in processes. The 5Rs focus on the Refinement, Reduction, Re-use, Recyclability and the Retrieval of energy throughout the company, by building in environmental considerations, minimising waste generation at source, re-using packaging, recycling material in the same or different processes and optimising energy resources. Toyota Manufacturing UK will continue to set itself challenging targets with key indicators used across the company to measure environmental performance focusing on reducing solvent emissions, waste requiring disposal, water and energy usage.

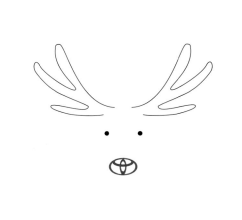

5

6

avensis
UK JAPAN EXPORT
CELEBRATION

7

Zero Design Limited

The Coach House / Northumberland Street South East Lane
Edinburgh EH3 6LP
T +44 (0)131 556 1333 / F +44 (0)131 556 3113
nobody@zero-design.net
www.zero-design.net

Management Lisa Jelley, Stuart Robins **Contact** Lisa Jelley
Staff 4 **Founded** 1998

Company Profile

Founded with the express purpose of offering our clients a
complete visual communication service – designing for
print, multimedia and the Internet – Zero has developed into
brand strategy experts, where designing and applying a
corporate image is approached in a fresh, creative way.

Our skills have been developed from working closely with a
number of significant marketing companies, taking the best
of a marketing approach and applying it to our designs, but
in a totally new and exciting way. Due to this, Zero are in a
unique position where they can offer a fresh approach to
your brand development requirements, be they in print or on
the web, utilising our design and marketing skills accrued
through years of experience in both camps.

What do we offer?

- Creative, strategic and technical services for corporate
  and brand communication
- Services for internal and external audiences
- On-line and off-line capabilities

Our creative services encompass structural packaging
and surface graphics, marketing collateral, print production,
annual reports, website development, cd-rom, corporate
graphics, brand image and tone-of-voice, brand naming
for new product development, brand and range
extensions/leverage products, interiors, vehicle livery,
exhibitions, signage and retail environments.

Our clients include

Albyn
Bank of Scotland
Carnegie Worldwide
The Edrington Group
ExxonMobil
Glenmorangie plc
The Open University
Pinnacle Telecoms plc
Rangers FC
Regular Music
Scottish Textiles
Sports Bar
University of Ulster

1 Lindores Abbey Limited Edition Whisky
2 Christmas Card and Gift Book for Lakeland Stores
3 Mixmasters FAB alcopop range
4 Bank of Scotland Premierleague, formerly the Scottish
  Premier League (SPL)
5 Pinnacle Telecoms plc re-brand
6 Rangers Racing Club for Rangers FC
7 Scotland IS formerly the Scottish Software Federation
8 Glenmorangie House 'Whisky Weekends' brochure
9 West Coast Harley-Davidson website

Beacon Creative Ltd

No1 Church Street / Tyne Bridge Approach
Gateshead NE8 2AT
T +44 (0)191 478 4411 / F +44 (0)191 478 7711
info@beaconcreative.com
www.beaconcreative.com

Contact Phil Moore
Staff 7 **Founded** 1998
Membership British Design & Art Direction

Some of the UK's most successful companies use our services for brand orientated Design. Indeed, 80% of our work is repeat business from many tried and tested market leaders.

Our clients invest millions of pounds developing and producing products that we've designed and ultimately we are judged by the bottom line. A lot of our work ends up competing in the market place on shelf. There's no room for error when dealing with the harshest critics of all – the consumer.

We are constantly trying to push ourselves and are proud to be trusted with taking some household names into new markets and brand extensions.

The majority of our work is focused on brand licensing. We create packaging graphics and concepts, literature, POP and Style guides. Promotional materials, catalogues, exhibitions and web sites.

We try to keep our company structure as flat as possible with a clear path from designer to client. We find our service is sharper this way. Our streamlined operation offers the client a direct route to what they are paying for, quality design.

Beacon has a clear goal, provide quality creative solutions to our clients. No jargon and no barriers.

1 Style guide – Royal Ballet
2 Packaging BBC Top Gear
3 Homer Simpson kitchen timer
4 Monsters Inc. table top range
5 Smiley Worldwide brand extension
6 Facial tissues packaging
7 Style guide – Disney

beacon creative ltd.

4

5

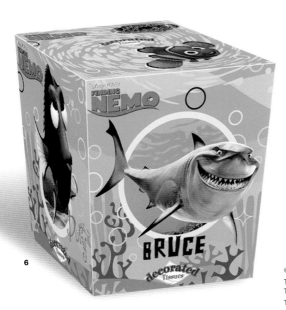

6

7

Blackburn's Ltd
Brand Design

16 Carlisle Street / London W1D 3BT
T +44 (0)20 7734 7646 / F +44 (0)20 7437 0017
caroline@blackburnsdesign.com
www.blackburnsdesign.com

Management John Blackburn, Belinda Duggan
Contact Caroline Newson
Founded 1969

Blackburn's, based in the heart of London's Soho, with
over thirty years experience in brand packaging design,
handling a broad international client base, for both large
multi-nationals and small independent companies.

Drinks are our speciality.

Our belief is that the strongest brand identities are those
built on a 'Big Idea'. Ideas drive creativity: they define a
brand's personality and are a key to commercial success.
Decorative graphics are not enough: to have any real
impact, packaging must be distinctive, emotive,
campaignable and ownable.

Our expertise includes NPD, brand reappraisal, structural
design, name generation, logo creation and supporting
promotional material. We offer a bespoke service to suit any
marketing strategy.

Over the past decade alone, Blackburn's have won over
100 major awards around the world for both creativity
(D&AD, Clio, Epica) and for design effectiveness (DBA,
Marketing and Drinks International).

Bloom Brand Design

25 The Village / 101 Amies Street / London SW11 2JW
T +44 (0)20 7924 4533 / F +44 (0)20 7924 4553
harriet@bloom-design.com
www.bloom-design.com

Management Gavin Blake, Harriet Marshall, Ben White
Contacts Harriet Marshall, Ben White
Staff 21 **Founded** 2001

Company Profile
Bloom is a compact design agency with three areas
of excellence:
Understanding
Creativity
Delivery

We seek to simplify rather than complicate and we don't
have any black box TM techniques. Our house style is bold,
simple and iconic, our spirit friendly.

Founded in 2001, we're young, independent and hungry.

Our Clients Include:
Associated Newspapers
Danone
Diageo
Disney
Nestle
Spy Publishing
Unilever

See also Branding and Graphic Design p. 24

Boxer

St Philip's Court / Church Hill / Coleshill
Birmingham B46 3AD
T +44 (0)1675 467 050 / F +44 (0)1675 465 288
paul@boxer.uk.com
www.boxer.uk.com

Also at: Brand Building / 14 James Street
London WC2E 8BU

See also Branding and Graphic Design p. 28

WWW.BOXER.UK.COM

Brewer Riddiford Design Consultants

69 Shelton Street / London WC2H 9HE
T +44 (0)20 7240 9351 / F +44 (0)20 7836 2897
george@brewer-ridd.co.uk
www.brewer-riddiford.co.uk

Contacts George Riddiford, Celine Smith
Staff 25 **Founded** 1992 **Membership** Design Business Association

Specialists in Brand Identity and Packaging Design
We are a group of 25 highly experienced design and marketing professionals, consistently delivering dramatic design solutions for heavyweight and demanding clients. We fervently believe in the central role played by brand design in building profitable brands.

Our senior partner team is made up of career designers and ex-client marketers, so we bring a healthy balance of perspectives to every problem.

Dramatic Solutions Well Thought Through
Over the past 12 years, we are proud to have been selected for a wide range of brand rejuvenations and new brand projects, each critically important to the success of the client company concerned.

These clients' faith in us has been rewarded by tangible, quantifiable sales results and plenty of creative and effectiveness awards, as well as inspiring many long-lasting relationships. More than 65% of our business today is with clients with whom we have worked since the early 1990s.

2003 Clients
Accantia Health & Beauty Ltd
Birds Eye Frozen Foods
Coca Cola GB
Diageo
Galbani
W Jordan (Cereals) Ltd
PC World
Riso Gallo SPA
Sainsburys
Thorntons

1   Oasis - Coca Cola GB & Ireland
2   Simple - Accantia Health & Beauty Ltd
3   Blossom Hill - Percy Fox Ltd & Co
4   Eden - Thorntons

Creative Edge
Design Consultants

Riverside House / Heron Way / Newham
Truro Cornwall TR1 2XN
T +44 (0)1872 260 023 / F +44 (0)1872 264 110
mail@creativeedge.co.uk
www.creativeedge.co.uk

Management Dave Rickett and Melinda Rickett
Contact Melinda Rickett
Staff 10 **Founded** 1992 **Membership** The Chartered
Society of Designers

Company Profile
We are a West-Country based, award-winning creative
design consultancy with over 25 years experience in design
solutions for local, national and international clients.

Clients
Duchy Originals
Highgrove
Kettle Produce
Univeg
Carmel
Coodes Solicitors
Cornish King
Cornwall College
Cornwall County Council
Cornwall Enterprise
Cornwall Tourism Board
British Telecom
Falmouth College of Art
Furniss Foods
Midas Construction
James Walker Group
National Maritime Museum Cornwall
South West Quality Meat
Pilchard Works
Callestick Ice Cream
Carley's Health Foods
Cyder Farm
Crantock Bakery
Fuddruckers
Soil Association
Sinclair Animal & Household Care
Swallowcourt Group
Doble Foods

Brand and product development for local, national
and international clients.

dare!
brand identity & packaging

3 East Causeway Close / Leeds LS16 8LN / West Yorkshire
T +44 (0)113 281 7080 / F +44 (0)113 281 7088
dare.smt@virgin.net
dareonline.co.uk

Contacts Debbie Seal, Simon Tame
Founded 1998

We are an award-winning consultancy, specialising in the conception and development of brands and packaging within the alcoholic beverage sector.

dare! has evolved as a result of producers' and importers' needs for a knowledgeable, sensible, yet creative approach that leads to effective design solutions.

We believe in developing very close working relationships with all our clients in order to achieve the best possible results. Being a small, 'hands-on' company allows us to adopt this much-appreciated approach.

Working on a diverse range of projects from evolutionary re-designs through to the creation and development of major new brands, our attention-to-detail is second to none.

Our expertise extends to the creation of advertising and support material which we see as a natural extension of our close involvement in the development of both new and existing brands.

dare!

wine sellers

Design Bridge
Branding and Packaging

18 Clerkenwell Close / London EC1R 0QN
T +44 (0)20 7814 9922 / F +44 (0)20 7814 9024
enquiries@designbridge.com
www.designbridge.com

Singapore Office / 5 Kadayanallur Street
Singapore 069183 / Singapore
T +65 6224 2336 / F +65 6224 2386
enquiries@designbridge.com
www.designbridge.com

Amsterdam Office / Keizersgracht 424
1016 GC Amsterdam / The Netherlands
T +31 (0)20 520 6030 / F +31 (0)20 520 6059
enquiries@designbridge.com
www.designbridge.com

Management Sir William Goodenough bt., Jill Marshall,
Nick Verebelyi **Contact** Jill Marshall
Staff 135 **Founded** 1986

At Design Bridge we believe brands are like people. They
come in all shapes and sizes, from the well-adjusted to
those with more deep-rooted problems and still more
waiting to be born. Whatever the scenario, we speak their
language and understand their needs. The common thread
is always fresh thinking, with every brief a new challenge.

Our particular strategic and creative skills can be used
individually, or in combination, to unlock the potential in
every brand. Whether the most compelling need for a new
corporate brand identity, promotional literature or a three-
dimensional expression of a brand, bespoke bottle or
graphic packaging, or even a digital media campaign, we
have over 15 years' experience helping companies around
the world to realise their goals, and those of their product
or service brands.

Packaging has to work especially hard, often at the
supermarket frontline where people make instant
judgements about brands, just as they do about people.
We also never forget that the view from behind is just as
important, and that every element of the pack must work
together to reinforce brand values. So how much more
powerful when surface graphics are combined with a
bespoke 3D form – optimising functionality and creating
a single-minded branding message.

See also Branding and Graphic Design p. 34

1 Punch & Judy Children's Toothpaste. A brand with
   over 20 years' heritage, redesigned for the 21st century.
   Bold colours and illustrations, entertaining and engaging
   young consumers. On behalf of Roche Products.
2 The Beer to Dine for. Challenging perceptions of beer,
   formulated to be enjoyed with food. Contemporary
   label design and a uniquely shaped bottle. Produced
   for Greene King.
3 Dulux Editions. A new range of contemporary paint
   colours and themes. Photographic images produce
   memorable can designs with amazing shelf standout.
   Designed for ICI Dulux.

1

2

insightful,
confident,
inspirational...

Dew Gibbons
create, revitalise and manage consumer brands

4º Tabernacle Street / London EC2A 4AA
T +44 (0)20 7689 8999 / F +44 (0)20 7689 9377
itsgreat@dewgibbons.com
www.dewgibbons.com

Management Shaun Dew, Steve Gibbons
Contacts Carol Lewin, Steve Gibbons
Staff 14 **Founded** 1997 **Memberships** CSD, BDI, D&AD,
DBA, DTI Trade Partners, RSA

With over 40 award wins in the last 5 years, Dew Gibbons
is one of the UK's leading creative design consultancies.
Our experience, knowledge, passion and enthusiasm
is focused towards excellence in consumer branding.

Selected Clients
BBC
Boots the Chemists
Coca-Cola
Cosmopolitan Cosmetics
De Beers LV
Forest Laboratories Europe
Julien Macdonald
Lindt & Sprungli
Pret A Manger
Procter & Gamble
Sara Lee
Vidal Sassoon

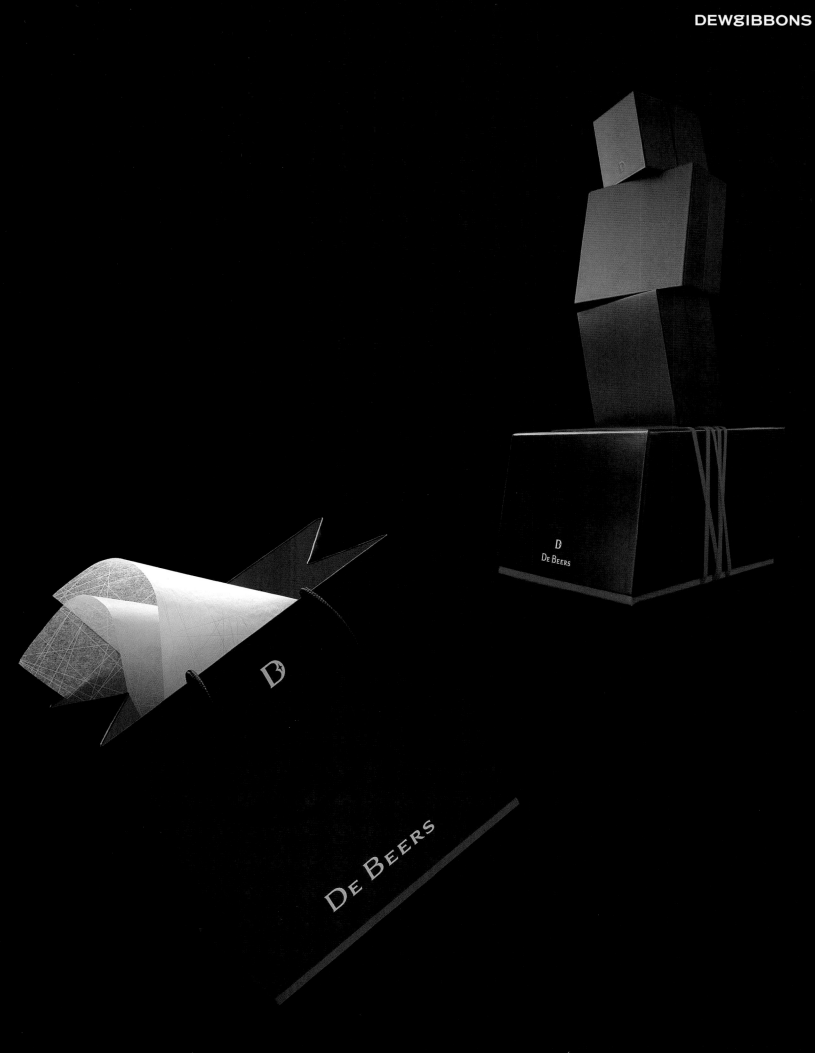

Enterprise IG
The Global Brand Design
Agency

11-33 St John Street / London EC1M 4PJ
T +44 (0)20 7559 7000 / F +44 (0)20 7559 7001
enquiries@enterpriseig.com
www.enterpriseig.co.uk

Contact Ms Robin Kadrnka, Group Marketing Director
Founded 1976

We've been around for over 25 years and are the world's
leading global brand design agency, employing some 650
people in 24 offices worldwide. Part of the WPP Group,
Enterprise IG develops brand design solutions for brand
owners globally, redefining categories, facilitating brand
stretch and engaging consumers.

Understanding the role of the product at point of purchase
as well as 'in use' ensures that our solutions maximise the
product experience for the consumer and deliver tangible
insights for our clients.

Our product branding programmes have delivered business
growth for brands such as Nestlé, Dove, Absolut, Coca-Cola,
Scrabble, Kelloggs, Andrex, Kodak, Pilsner Urquell, Johnnie
Walker, Mr. Kipling and Sun Silk.

**See also Branding and Graphic Design p. 38 and Interior,
Retail and Event Design p. 182**

1 Boots 17 Molton Metals
2 Caol Ila 18 Year Old Whisky
3 Vodafone Packaging Design
4 Tian Tey Packaging and Brand Manual

1

2

3

4

Hurricane Design
Consultants Ltd

32 Cambray Place / Cheltenham GL50 1JP
T +44 (0)1242 222 860 / F +44 (0)1242 216 768
david@hurricanedesign.com
www.hurricanedesign.co.uk

Contact David Myerson
Staff 12 **Founded** 1997

Company Profile
It's all too easy to talk about our strong sense of belief
in brands, our commitment to the creative process and
how we integrate graphic and structural packaging design
to deliver a successful brand strategy. Ultimately it's
the consumer who decides what's good and what isn't,
but until then, it's your decision.

Clients
Acco
Aldi
Coca-Cola
Costa
Dawn Foods
Kenwood
Kraft Foods
Matthew Clark
Pretty Polly
Sara Lee
Seagrams
Spontex
United Biscuits
United Distillers
Wella

Radox
Herbal therapy for Sara Lee. We have been evolving
the Radox brand for around 8 years, bringing new life
and invigoration to a UK brand leader.

Morgan's Spiced Gold
Adding a touch of spice to Seagrams. A brand extension
for Morgan's rum.

Derwent Pencils
Wrapping up the finest pencils for Acco. Developing
packaging which is a product in its own right. And not a tin
in sight.

Matey
Splash out on the kids. Bringing fun to bath time for
Sara Lee.

Dr Pepper
This is not a Cola. Creation of a bottle form which defines
the brand category.

Radox
SARA LEE

Morgan's Spiced
SEAGRAMS

Derwent Pencils
ACCO

Matey
SARA LEE

Dr. Pepper
COCA COLA

Indigo Partnership
International
Brand Architects

35a Laitwood Road / London SW12 9QN / Balham
T +44 (0)208 772 0185 / T +44 (0)7801 688 957
F +44 (0)208 772 0561
kevin@indigopartners.co.uk
www.indigopartners.co.uk

Management Kevin McGurk, Sarah Kellaghan, Bob Grierson
Contact Kevin McGurk
Staff 10 **Founded** 1998

Realising Brand Potential

Behind every 'champion' is a dedicated team of professionals whose experience and objective advice builds on the competitor's unique strengths, minimises their weaknesses, constantly honing their skills to create a competitive edge.

We believe developing brands to become winners is no less challenging.

Successful brands don't just happen, they are driven by a determination to fulfil a potential opportunity not yet realised.

Indigo Partnership International, has thirty years of experience developing successful brand strategies for our clients. We work in a discreet and collaborative way to bring objective insights that deliver real competitive advantage.

Our aim is to help you achieve your business objectives through consistent brand performance, market share growth and improved bottom-line profitability.

Effective branding is about winning, not just participating.

Clients

Boots Healthcare International
B&Q – Planet Diamond Tools
Ferrero – Tic Tac
Mac Baren Pipe Tobacco
Marks & Spencer
Masterfoods – Whiskas
Pågen Bakery
Swedish Match – Borkum Riff,
Vin & Sprit – Absolut

See also Branding and Graphic Design p. 48

1 Bryant & May, Swedish Match
2 Borkum Riff, Pipe Tobacco, Swedish Match
3 General Whisky, Swedish Match

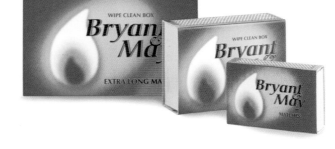

jones knowles ritchie

128 Albert Street / London NW1 7NE
T +44 (0)20 7428 8000 / F +44 (0)20 7428 8080
info@jkr.co.uk
www.jkr.co.uk

Winning in a 1-Second World
There are 25,000 items in the average supermarket, yet only 55 go into the average shopping trolley. And only 75 minutes to choose them in.

Impulse purchasing drives your brands' success.

Fight commoditisation with distinctive and engaging design! Design that puts the brand first, not the consumer, so it can't be 'adapted' by your friends at the supermarkets.

Nice theory, but does it work in practice? Send a blank email to katygale@jkr.co.uk and we'll send you some data, so you can judge for yourself.

Principal Clients
Bacardi
Britvic
Heinz
Interbrew
Mars
Molton Brown

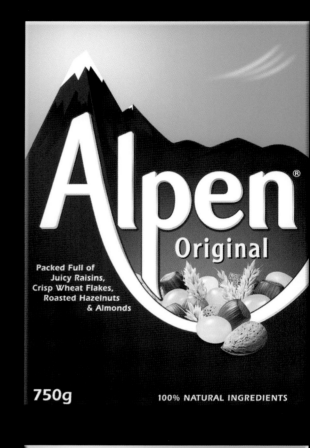

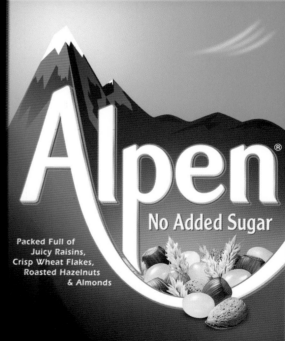

jkr

jones knowles ritchie

DESIGN SOLUTIONS

ANDY KNOWLES :
020 7428 8000 www.jkr.co.uk

Navyblue Design Group

122 Giles Street / Edinburgh EH6 6BZ
T +44 (0)131 553 5050 / F +44 (0)131 555 0707
edinburgh@navyblue.com
www.navyblue.com

Third Floor Morelands / 17-21 Old Street
London EC1V 9HL
T +44 (0)20 7253 0316 / F +44 (0)20 7553 9409
london@navyblue.com
www.navyblue.com

Management Douglas Alexander, Managing Director
Navyblue Scotland, Geoff Nicol, Managing Director
Navyblue London
Contacts Mike Lynch, Business Development Director,
Toby Southgate, Client Services Director
Staff 68 **Founded** 1994

Company Profile

Navyblue's core business is creative design and
communications, supported by internal strategic planning
and research – one of our values is "thinking out louder™",
and this approach influences everything we do. Since 1994
we have expanded our skill-set from traditional graphics into
the areas of 3d environments and new media, incorporating
technical development expertise as well as on-screen
design capability. Navyblue is one of the UK's top 30 design
consultancies, employing more than 65 people and with
a turnover in excess of £7 million.

Packaging

Creating fresh and impactful packaging is a core branding
element for all manner of consumer offerings. Equally as
important are one-off projects for new product launches,
unique product offers or specific events. Our experience
in packaging design covers the drinks sector, health and
beauty products, ambient foods, and point-of-purchase
brand expression. What underpins all these projects is the
thinking and strategy that enables us to deliver a core
objective for our client – whether it's breaking into a new
market, increasing seasonal sales, or simply celebrating
a new vintage of a favourite malt.

Clients

Baxters Fresh Soup – packaging campaign,
new product launch
Baxters Nick Nairn Range – packaging campaign,
new product launch
Baxters Noodle Soup – packaging campaign,
new product launch
Boots – giftcard packaging
Body Shop – seasonal packaging campaigns
Ellesse – in-store displays, product packaging,
point-of-purchase material
Orange – product packaging, student and youth
propositions

See also Branding and Graphic Design p. 64, New Media
Design p. 160 and Interior, Retail and Event Design p. 194

1 Boots giftcard range packaging
2 Baxters Fresh Soup packaging
3 Baxters Nick Nairn Pan Fry Sauce packaging

1

2

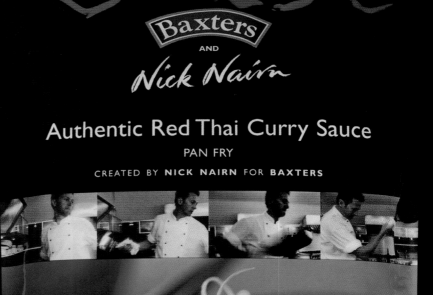

3

Osborne Pike

Bath Brewery / Toll Bridge Road / Bath BA1 7DE
T +44 (0)1225 851 551
steve@osbornepike.co.uk
www.osbornepike.co.uk

Management Steve Osborne, David Pike, David Rivett
Contacts Steve Osborne, David Pike
Staff 4 **Founded** 2002

Company Profile
Osborne Pike is the consultancy that gives clients what
it says on the label: Steve Osborne and David Pike.

We have between us over 30 years of experience in the
branding game, gained with some of its most successful
practitioners.

We provide design and consultancy for a small number
of high-powered clients.

Clients
Douwe Egberts
Campbell Grocery Products
Heineken
Sara Lee

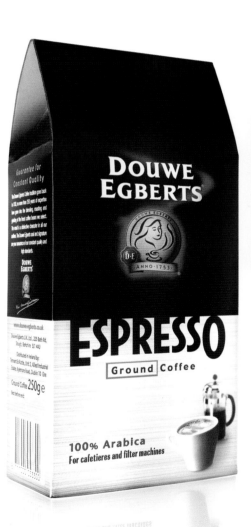

PDD
The Innovation Partner

85-87 Richford Street / London W6 7HJ
T +44 (0)20 8735 1111 / F +44 (0)20 8735 1133
info@pdd.co.uk
www.pdd.co.uk

Management Helen Gray **Contacts** Mark Tosey,
Lara Hawketts
Staff 80 **Founded** 1978 **Memberships** RCA, CSD,
D&AD, IDSA
Recent design awards D&AD, IDSA, Red Dot

"Number one product design consultancy 2003"
Design Week Creative League Survey – Top 100 Design
Groups

PDD is one of the UK's largest product and packaging
design consultancies, with over twenty years' international
experience.

We know that successful brands are built by integrating
human insight, creativity and technical knowledge.
At PDD this blend of expertise comes under one roof.

Our unique on-site research and technology facility gives
you access to a new type of innovation partner. One that
harnesses fresh thinking and gives outstanding solutions.
Our vibrant, inventive culture focuses on the complete
packaging cycle from strategic research and visioning,
through detailed design, to full implementation ready for
manufacture and launch.

When it comes to packaging innovation, we deliver the
tangible difference.

Pure
Packaging & Brand

4 The Heritage Centre / High Pavement / The Lace Market
Nottingham NG1 1HN / Nottinghamshire
T +44 (0)115 958 2107 / M +44 (0)7989 322 304
F +44 (0)115 950 4948
david@purebydesign.co.uk
www.purebydesign.co.uk

Management David Rogers, Sue Allsopp
Contact David Rogers
Staff 11 **Founded** 1999

Pure was founded 5 years ago with a simple concept in mind: to create distinctive designs that have soul and generate strong positive customer responses.

Our company culture is to be approachable and passionate and to listen to clients.

Clients' design problems become our opportunities.

If you have a problem you would like to share, please contact David Rogers on +44 (0)115 958 2107.

1 Breville - Laughter Lines, packaging and brand design
2 Trevor Sorbie - Global Haircare, development of brand and packaging
3 Nicky Clarke Electrical - range relaunch, structual, graphic and brand development
4 Boots The Chemists - 17 Christmas gift range, colour and packaging development

a bit of cheek

CLIENTS MARKS & SPENCER•TREVOR SORBIE VOLVO•BREVILLE•BOOTS•NICKY CLARKE•PHILIPS

David Rogers, Director "Pure was built out of a frustration for real creative without the stigma of high fees and client sweeteners. All we want to do is help you to sell your brands through excellent design. Our clients are as varied as the work we produce. If small is beautiful, then I would say that Pure is f***ing gorgeous".

a
lot of
talent

1   2   3   4

PACKAGING | ADVERTISING | CORPORATE LITERATURE | BRAND IDENTITY | DIRECT MARKETING | WEB DESIGN

pure

R Design

Studio 3, Church Studios / Camden Park Road
London NW1 9AY
T +44 (0)20 7284 5840 / F +44 (0)20 7284 5849
dave@r-email.co.uk
www.r-website.co.uk

Management David Richmond
Staff 5 **Founded** 1990

Company Profile
R Design offers a shopping list of creativity, including:
Raw talent
Graphic identity
Sauce
Own-label
Bubbly
Packaging
Freshener
Tasty work
Ginger nuts
Clean & Clear
No Spam

Clients
Debenhams
Selfridges
Sportzone (Portugal)
Bennet (Italy)
Tesco
The Food Doctor
WH Smith
Woolworths

See also Branding and Graphic Design p. 74

Seachange Creative Partners

The Coda Centre / 189 Munster Road / London SW6 6AW
T +44 (0)207 385 5656
nicky@seachangecreative.com
www.seachangecreative.com

Company Profile
Our aim is to work in partnership with our clients to deliver
outstanding creative solutions and to keep their brands at
the forefront of the public's mind.

We achieve this by staying true to our values:

Experienced, senior people will manage your business,
personally.

Our creative process is interactive, inspiring and fun!

We take time to understand your company culture, listen
to your consumers and get to the roots of your brands.

In striving for creative excellence we always challenge
along the way.

We balance creativity with pragmatism to achieve truly
effective results.

Clients
Adidas
Big Thoughts
Coty Lancaster
Freixenet
GlaxoSmithKline
L'Oréal
Nutrinnovator
The Tussauds Group

1 Altú – wrapping a new range of naturally nutritious and
  delicious food bars
2 Freixenet – putting the sparkle back into Vintage Cava
  and cultivating a new still wine range, Ash Tree Estate
3 Lucozade – energising a seventy-five-year-old, great
  British brand

Springetts

13 Salisbury Place / London W1H 1FJ
T +44 (0)20 7486 7527 / F +44 (0)20 7487 3033
all@springetts.co.uk
www.springetts.co.uk

Management Andy Black, Roger Bannister
Contact Brendan Thorpe
Staff 41

Company Profile
As one of the UK's top independently owned branding and
design consultancies, Springetts has a range of clients from
small and local to big and global. Our extensive expertise
in packaging design is demonstrated in the range and
longevity of many of our client relationships. Our honesty
and integrity allow us to build strong working partnerships
where clients deal directly with strategically literate
designers, not account handlers.

See also Branding and Graphic Design p. 84

1 Radnor Hills Mineral Water Company, Heartsease
   Mineral Water: structural design, graphic design,
   branding
2 Dairy Crest, Gold Low Fat Spread: graphic design
3 Sara Lee Household & Body Care, Ambi-Pur Radiante:
   structural design, pack design, graphic design, branding
4 Dairy Crest, Cathedral City: structural design, graphic
   design, branding
5 Young's Bluecrest, Young'uns: pack design, graphic
   design, branding
6 Twinings International, fruit-flavoured black tea: pack
   design, graphic design
7 Twinings UK, fruit infusions: pack design, graphic design

142

Springetts.co.uk

Brand Positioning

Naming

Brand & Corporate Identity

Structural Design

N.P.D

Licensing

1

2

3

4

5

6

7

TWININGS
INFUSIONS
RASPBERRY
STRAWBERRY &
LOGANBERRY
FLAVOUR TEABAGS
*A blend of soft
English fruits.*
20
TEABAGS   40g

TWININGS
INFUSIONS
LEMON
BURST
FLAVOUR TEABAGS
*An invigorating infusion with
a zesty lemon tang.*
20
TEABAGS   NET WT 40g

TWININGS
INFUSIONS
BLACKCURRANT
BURST
FLAVOUR TEABAGS
*Full of the taste of ripe
blackcurrants.*
20
TEABAGS   40g

TWININGS
INFUSIONS
CAMOMILE
& SPEARMINT
FLAVOUR TEABAGS
*A calming infusion with
a refreshing taste.*
20
TEABAGS   NET WT 30g

TWININGS
INFUSIONS
LEMON
& GINGER
FLAVOUR TEABAGS
*A warming drink with
a citrus tang.*
20
TEABAGS   NET WT 30g

Start Creative Limited

2 Sheraton Street / Soho / London W1F 8BH
T +44 (0)20 7269 0101 / F +44 (0)20 7269 0102
jen@startcreative.co.uk
startcreative.co.uk

Management Mike Curtis, Darren Whittingham,
Jennifer McAleer, Ian Kempen **Contact** Jennifer McAleer
Staff 59 **Founded** 1996

Company Profile
We're in the business of ideas and creativity. Here, we think
differently and this makes Start an exciting place to be.

Start is a creative agency with one aim – to deliver inspiring
creativity to meet business needs. We have burning passion
for three things – branding, marketing and digital media.
We specialise, we integrate and we deliver, using five sets
of skills – strategy, design, writing, production, and project
management.

We have enjoyed eight years of progressive growth. Now
we are the 10th largest independent creative agency in the
UK. Our clients include some of Britain's best brands. Last
year we won numerous effectiveness awards. We attract
and nurture some 60 of the industry's most talented people,
whose creative minds are dedicated to the needs of our
clients.

Clients
Virgin
BBC
Royal Mail
Hertz
Ordnance Survey
Interserve plc
Thetrainline
uSwitch
Land Registry
Nelsonbach
Transport for London
Department of Health
COI Communications
UK Trade & Investment
Fox Williams
Cisco Systems
Azzurri

**See also Branding and Graphic Design p. 86,
New Media Design p. 166 and Interior, Retail and
Event Design p. 202**

1   Spatone European branding and packaging
2   Virgin Pulse branding and packaging

Brand development   Marketing   Digital Media   Integrated   International

1

2

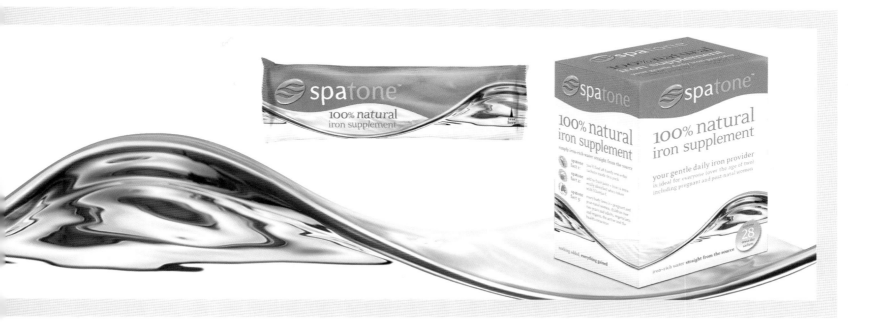

Two by Two
Design Consultants

348 Goswell Road / London EC1V 7LQ
T +44 (0)20 7278 1122 / F +44 (0)20 7278 1155
zebra@twobytwo.co.uk
www.twobytwo.co.uk

Management Ashwin Shaw , Salvatore Cicero
Contacts Ashwin Shaw, Salvatore Cicero
Staff 12 **Founded** 1995

Company Profile
Blah blah blah blah blah blah blah blah
blah blah blah blah blah blah blah blah
blah blah blah . . .

... originality breeds content

Clients include
Couture Brands
Dudley plc
Elemis London Ltd
Europa Office
Magnelli
L'Oreal
Richard Ward
Royal Mint
J Sainsbury plc
Satyajit Ray Foundation
Teenage Cancer Trust
The Wine Society
Verco

See also Branding and Graphic Design p. 92

1   Richard Ward Haircare Range

146

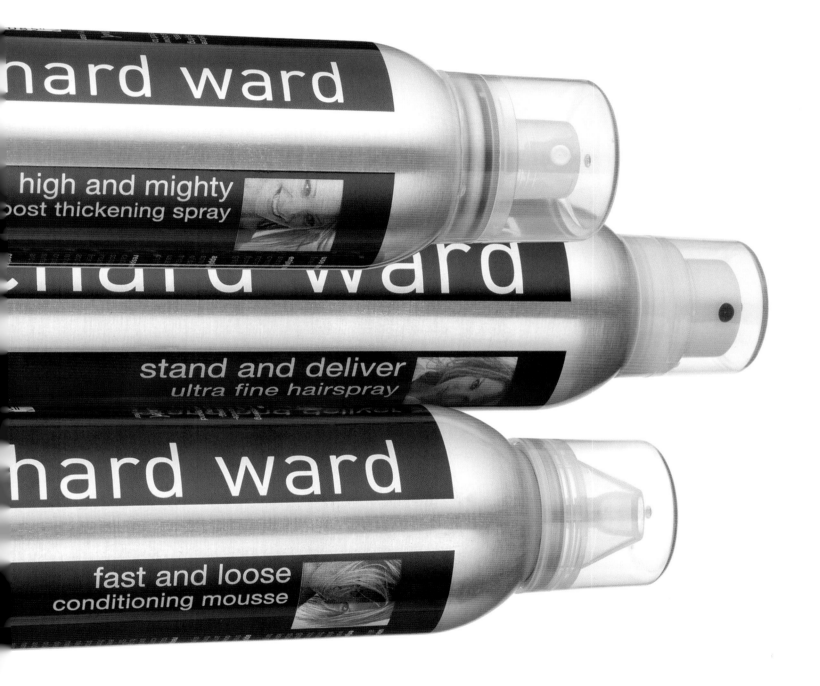

Watt
Strategic Brand Specialists

Watt UK / Ring Road / West Park / Leeds LS16 6RA
T +44 (0)113 288 3210 / F +44 (0)113 275 6044
info@whatswatt.co.uk
www.whatswatt.co.uk

Watt International / 300 Bayview Avenue
Toronto / Ontario / Canada M5A 3R7
T +1 416 364 9384 / F +1 416 363 1098
contactus@wattinternational.com
www.wattinternational.com

Company Profile
We are straight-talking, hard-hitting brand specialists.

From packaging design to complete brand architecture,
we have the capabilities and expertise to deliver profitable
business and design solutions.

If it's creative thinking you want without the bullshit, we're it.

See also Interior, Retail and Event Design p. 206

1   Blackcurrant Drink, Asda, UK
2   Appliance Packaging, General Electric,
    Canada, USA, Mexico
3   Progress Toddler Infant Milk, SMA, UK
4   Get Fruity Shower Gel, Asda, UK
5   Love Hearts, Swizzels Matlow, Global

Etu Odi Design
brand, print, digital

4 Pear Tree Court / London EC1R 0DS
T +44 (0)20 7689 9222 / F +44 (0)20 7689 9235
info@etuodi.co.uk
www.etuodi.co.uk

The Way It Is
We set off on our journey and soon discovered that our point of difference was a unique skill in speaking to the consumer in clear and concise tones – direct and to the point when required, or with wit and humour where this will achieve better results.

Creativity is our tool of choice in delivering both effective and award-winning graphic design and interactive projects for our clients.

Our Clients Include
British Film Institute – /print/interactive/
Esso – /print/retail/
Gloucester Road Smile Centre – /brand/print/web/
HP – /print/retail/
IBM – /print/
Mobay Restaurant – /brand/print/web/
Orange – /retail/print/
Pall Mall Pictures – /brand/print/web/
Penrose Housing Association – /brand/print/web/
Peugeot – /print/web/
Plant Food and Drink – /brand guardian/retail/web/
Silverstring – /brand/print/interactive/
Sony – /print/

1 Peugeot – HDi website
   www.peugeot.co.uk/hdi
   We looked to focus on the benefits rather than the technology in Peugeot's new generation diesel injection engines.
2 Silverstring – Website
   www.silverstring.com
   The message is wrapped in entertainment, leaving you charmed and informed.
3 Silverstring – CD-Rom
   Communicating the robustness and simplicity of Silverstring's new software appliance.
4 British Film Institute – Educational CD-Rom
   Used to stimulate discussion and aid projects on the early years of cinema in Britain.
5 Plant Food & Drink – Website
   www.plantfooddrink.co.uk
   The site was intended to showcase the brand of this vegetarian restaurant chain, being deliciously fresh and stylish.

Etu Odi Design

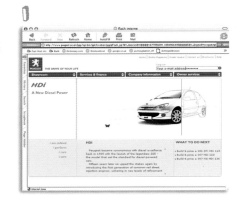

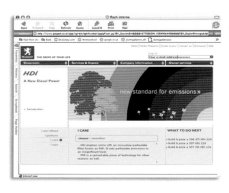

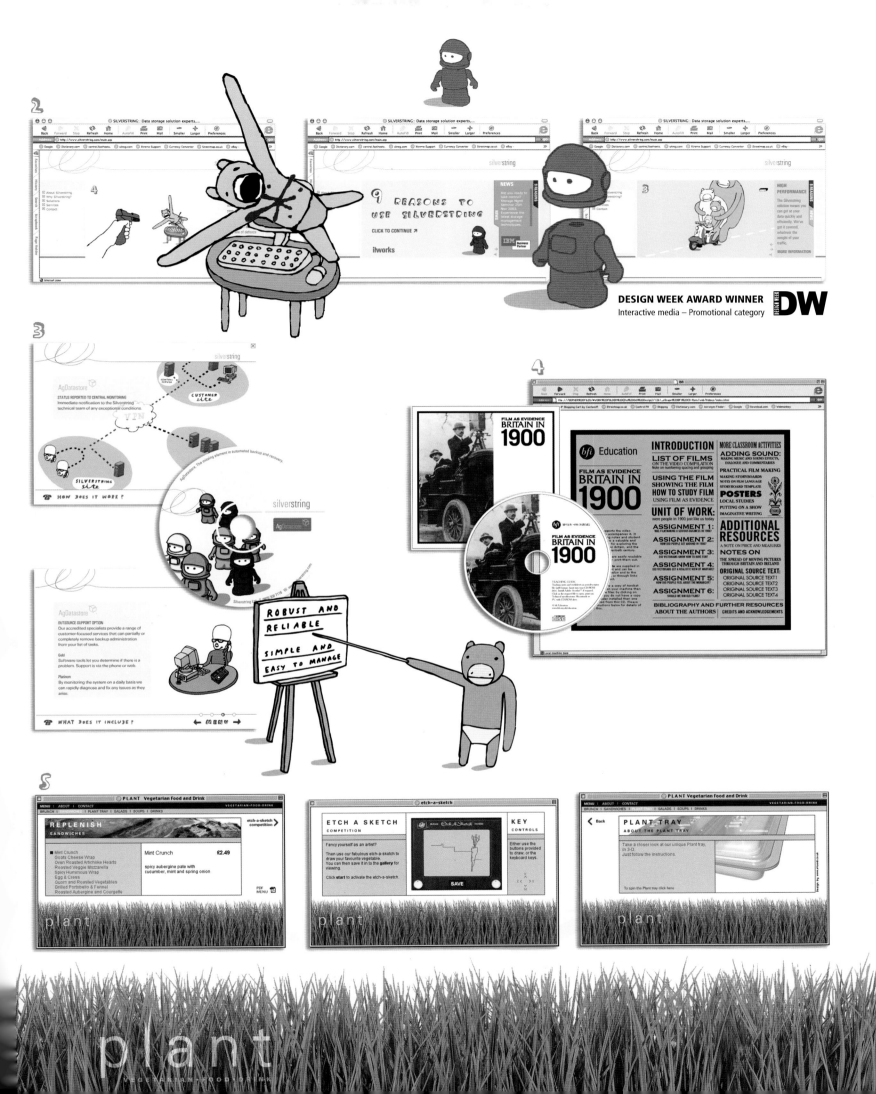

DESIGN WEEK AWARD WINNER DW
Interactive media – Promotional category

FUSEBOXDESIGN Ltd
We Are New Media

St Nicholas Chare / Newcastle upon Tyne NE1 1RJ
Tyne & Wear
T + 44 (0)191 245 7101 / F + 44 (0)191 245 7111
info@fuseboxdesign.co.uk
www.fuseboxdesign.co.uk

Management Sarah Linley, Louise Taylor, Jarrod Cocksedge
Contact Jarrod Cocksedge
Staff 6 **Founded** 2001

Company Profile
FUSEBOXDESIGN apply innovation and creativity to all our
design projects and believe in the highest standards of
usability and accessibility. We pride ourselves on helping
our clients identify their current and future requirements.
Our bespoke New Media solutions will give your business
the tools to manage change, make connections and
communicate with clients, partners and colleagues more
effectively.

Our broad and constantly expanding range of services
includes website and database design and development,
graphic design, corporate branding, search engine
optimisation, content management systems, animation,
e-mail marketing, IT consultancy and tailored training.

Clients
Chorister School
Desco
Durham City Council
Durham Constabulary
Sir Robert McAlpine
Newcastle City Council
One NorthEast
Red Box Design Group
Red Box Gallery
Sunderland City Council
Terrace Hill

1   www.fuseboxdesign.co.uk
2   www.redboxdesigngroup.com
3   Durham Constabulary Intranet
4   www.durham.police.uk
5   www.redboxgallery.com
6   www.fbdseo.com
7   Sunderland Arc

1

2

3

4

5

6

7

154

FUSEBOXDESIGN ▮▮ ▮

WEB DESIGN | GRAPHIC DESIGN | BRANDING | NEW MEDIA DESIGN

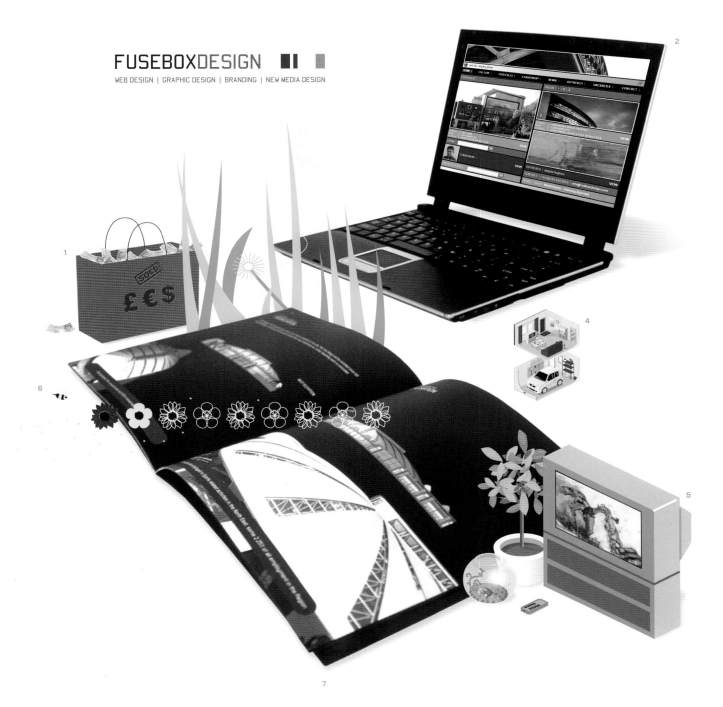

Kiwi

Effective new media communications

96 Broad Street / Birmingham B15 1AU
T +44 (0)121 688 8881
birmingham@kiwi.co.uk
www.kiwi.co.uk

2 Millharbour / Docklands / London E14 9TE
T +44 (0)20 7750 9940
london@kiwi.co.uk
www.kiwi.co.uk

Contacts John White, Terri Smart
Staff 14 **Founded** 1996

Kiwi began life in the mid-1990s when digital media was beginning to make a real impact.

We have always treated digital media as means of delivery for messages, not as messages themselves. What is true of all other media is true for digital: they must work efficiently and support the message, without getting in the way of content and creativity, which are what really matter.

We think we have the balance right, reflected in an impressive portfolio of internationally recognised work for international corporations, prominent UK businesses and public institutions.

Our experience, knowledge, insights, creativity and technical excellence mean that we can develop advanced digital media solutions, from campaign websites to enterprise information portals, which deliver significant and lasting benefits to our clients.

See also Branding and Graphic Design p. 52

See also Branding and Graphic Design p. 52

156

MP3
Zutons – You
You Wo

redi
fmg2.ram

PDF
Adobe
app form

Macintosh

bmit

GIF
fw
submit button.gif

EPS 9
CHOSEN LOGO.eps

e
Internet Expl

s – shoot
ligan mix)

styles.jsp

movies static 6.fla

MACSHARE

ons –
amac

the best EVER

kiwi

iTunes alias

xt

wallpaper

RealOne Player

s

MP3
lil' louie – french kiss

JPG
fw
home page.jpg

Dreamweaver MX 20

JPG
fw
kronicle.jpg

'curiosity is the key to creativity'
Akio Morita (1921 -)
www.kiwi.co.uk/curious

Lloyd Northover
Vivid brands, engaging experiences

2 Goodge Street / London W1T 2QA
T +44 (0)20 7420 4850 / F +44 (0)20 7420 4858
neil.hudspeth@lloydnorthover.com
www.lloydnorthover.com

Contacts Jim Northover, Neil Hudspeth
Founded 1975 **Memberships** DBA, D&AD, CSD, BDI

Company Profile
Lloyd Northover is a team of bright, inventive, down-to-earth people devoted to creating memorable and engaging brand experiences – across traditional and digital media, in two dimensions and three. At the heart of the company is our belief that design has the power to make a real difference to business and society, and to produce tangible returns on money spent. It's what we call creative value.

We attribute our enduring success to adeptness with new technologies, high creative standards, an analytical framework, disciplined project management and an insightfulness born of three decades. All of which enables us to strike the right balance between analytical and inspired, measured and daring.

Online or offline, our aim is to help brands perform. To produce interactive strategies and experiences that are individual to each client, our specialist digital consultants get under the skin of the business and brand issues, the audience needs, and the market and channel context.

Our interactive services include research and analysis, strategic e-business and brand consultancy, web services, content and application development, interface design and development, DiTV, channel and brand management, and e-marketing.

If you like what you see here, do get in touch and we'll tell you more about what we've done, who we've done it for and how we can do it for you.

Clients
APU (Anglia Polytechnic University)
Bank of America Capital Partners Europe
Barbican
Blue Sky Holidays Direct
BNFL
British Council
Continental Airlines
Financial Services Authority
Freeserve
Home Office
Invesco Perpetual
JMC Holidays
Legal & General Ventures
Mercury Direct
Messer Group (Germany)
NHS
Sunspot Tours
Taylor Woodrow
Welsh Development Agency

See also Branding and Graphic Design p. 54

Lloyd Northover

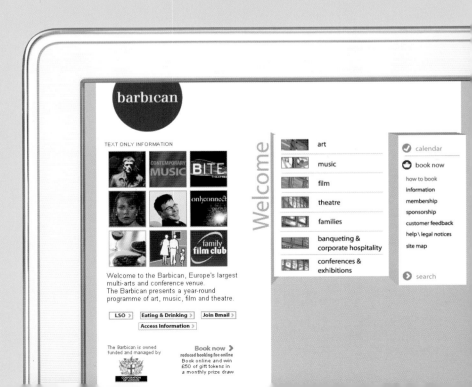

Navyblue Design Group

122 Giles Street / Edinburgh EH6 6BZ
T +44 (0)131 553 5050 / F +44 (0)131 555 0707
edinburgh@navyblue.com
www.navyblue.com

Third Floor Morelands / 17-21 Old Street
London EC1V 9HL
T +44 (0)20 7253 0316 / F +44 (0)20 7553 9409
london@navyblue.com
www.navyblue.com

Management Douglas Alexander, Managing Director
Navyblue Scotland, Geoff Nicol, Managing Director
Navyblue London
Contacts Mike Lynch, Business Development Director,
Toby Southgate, Client Services Director
Staff 68 **Founded** 1994

Company Profile
Navyblue's core business is creative design and
communications, supported by internal strategic planning
and research – one of our values is "thinking out louder™",
and this approach influences everything we do. Since 1994
we have expanded our skill-set from traditional graphics into
the areas of 3d environments and new media, incorporating
technical development expertise as well as on-screen
design capability. Navyblue is one of the UK's top 30 design
consultancies, employing more than 65 people and with
a turnover in excess of £7 million.

New Media
Navyblue's new media output fuses design-led
creativity with a deep technical grounding to produce a
comprehensive array of cross-platform solutions for all our
clients' digital needs. Our offering focuses on creating and
developing online brand identities across all new media
channels including eBrochures, eCommerce, Intranets,
Extranets, CD-ROM, email marketing, mobile technologies
and audio visual presentations.

Clients
Bank of Scotland – homepage springboard developed
in flash
Bond Advertising – cutting edge B2B website developed
in flash
Business Design Centre – B2C website design and
integration
English National Opera – website design and development
Hilton Group – annual report 2004 designed and
developed in flash
Ideal Standard – B2C website design
Knoll – knollknet: extranet design and development
Miller Homes – multi award winning B2C website featuring
bespoke CMS, eCRM and eDM campaigns
MTV – flash games design and development
Norwich Union Cars – on brand B2C eCommerce website
Scottish Courage – interactive B2B sales applications
Tune Up – AAA accessibility rated website for Scottish
Arts Council

See also Branding and Graphic Design p. 64, Packaging
Design p. 130 and Interior, Retail and Event Design p. 194

1 bond advertising website: www.bondadvertising.com
2 Ideal Standard website: www.thebathroom.info
3 Miller Homes website: www.millerhomes.co.uk
4 Scottish Arts Council – Tune Up website:
   www.tuneup.org.uk
5 Knoll Extranet

1

2

3

5

4

Oyster Partners Ltd
Interactive brand experiences

1 Naoroji Street / London WC1X 0JD
T +44 (0)20 7446 7500 / F +44 (0)20 7446 7555
Luke@oyster.com
www.oyster.com

Management Luke Taylor, Mike Mulligan, David Warner,
Deborah Keay, Nat Billington, Lorenzo Wood, Michael Khan
Contact Luke Taylor
Staff 96 **Founded** 1992

Oyster has been delivering innovative digital solutions for
clients since 1992. With projects ranging from brand
consultancy, through mobile and web interface
development, to enterprise-wide technical build, we have
unparalleled experience in ensuring that brands are
appropriately brought alive through all interactive channels.

Oyster combines marketing, business, technical and
creative expertise with an understanding of human
behaviour to design brand-led experiences across all digital
touchpoints. Working collaboratively with our clients and
partners, we pride ourselves on delivering accountable and
measurable solutions that satisfy the needs of our clients
and delight their customers.

Mercedes-Benz Lucky Star
Helping Mercedes-Benz bring their innovative
Lucky Star campaign to life online. Oyster's
work was accountable for 3,000 test drives
booked over three weeks.

Clifford Chance
Bringing the brand of the world's largest law firm alive for clients,
employees and prospects with a fresh new online identity which is

Orange
Creating innovative mobile interfaces, developing an inspiring
digital brand resource tool and implementing successful
strategies for marketing Orange's next generation services.

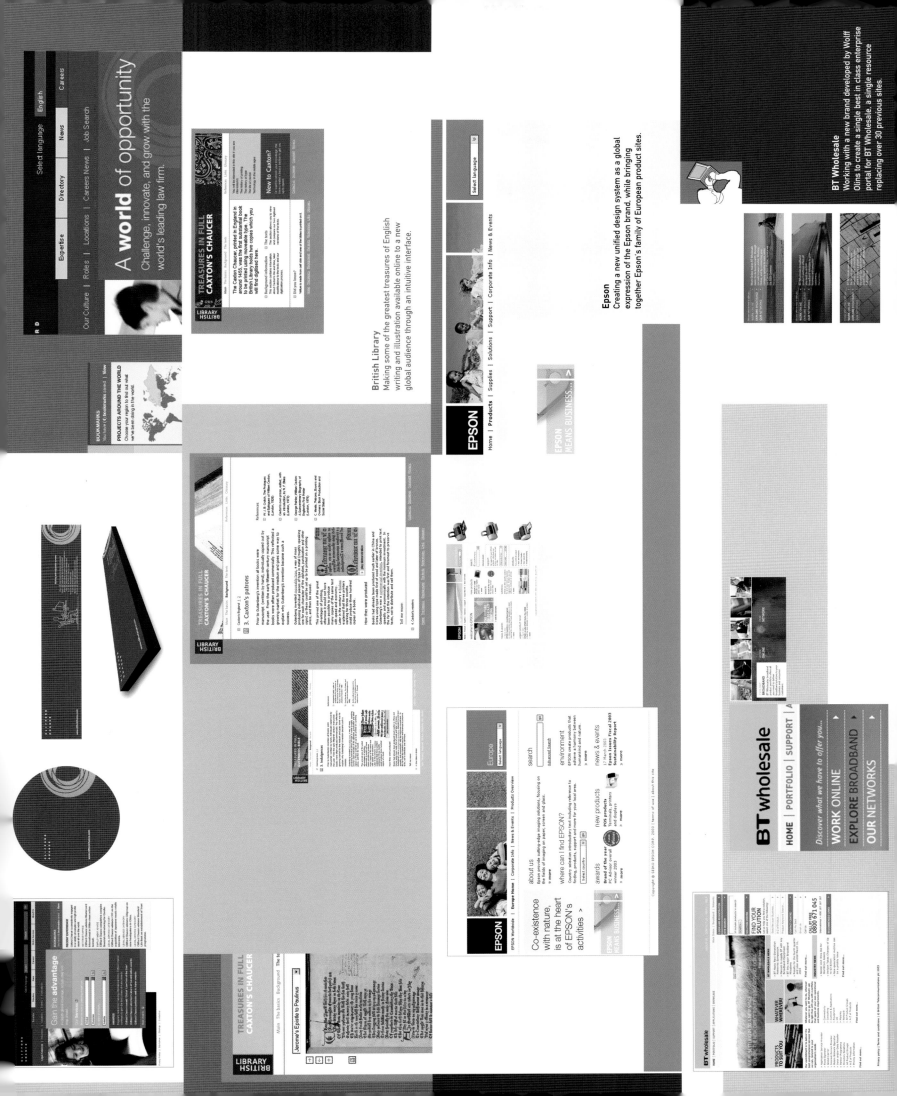

British Library
Making some of the greatest treasures of English writing and illustration available online to a new global audience through an intuitive interface.

Epson
Creating a new unified design system as a global expression of the Epson brand, while bringing together Epson's family of European product sites.

BT Wholesale
Working with a new brand developed by Wolff Olins to create a single best in class enterprise portal for BT Wholesale, a single resource replacing over 30 previous sites.

Spin

12 Canterbury Court / 1-3 Brixton Road / Kennington Park
London SW9 6DE
T +44 (0)20 7793 9555 / F +44 (0)20 7793 9666
patricia@spin.co.uk
www.spin.co.uk

Management Patricia Finegan, Tony Brook
Contact Patricia Finegan
Staff 11 **Founded** 1992 **Memberships** British Design & Art
Direction, Design Business Association

Company Profile
Established in 1992, Spin work across a variety of areas
including branding, print, retail, broadcast and moving
image. Spin's approach delivers clear communicative work
with strong concepts.

Clients
British Council
Caruso St John
Central Office of Information
Channel 4 Broadcasting
Christies
Deutsche Bank
Diesel
Five Broadcasting
Greater London Authority
Haunch of Venison
Health Education Authority
Ileana Makri
Levi Strauss & Co
MTV
Nike
Nokia
Orange
Photographer's Gallery
Precise Reprographics
Project 2
Rankin
Tate Modern
UBS
Vision-On Publishing
VH-1
Whitechapel Gallery

See also Branding and Graphic Design p. 80

Start Creative Limited

2 Sheraton Street / Soho / London W1F 8BH
T +44 (0)20 7269 0101 / F +44 (0)20 7269 0102
jen@startcreative.co.uk
startcreative.co.uk

Management Mike Curtis, Darren Whittingham,
Jennifer McAleer, Ian Kempen **Contact** Jennifer McAleer
Staff 59 **Founded** 1996

Company Profile
We're in the business of ideas and creativity. Here, we think
differently and this makes Start an exciting place to be.

Start is a creative agency with one aim – to deliver inspiring
creativity to meet business needs. We have burning passion
for three things – branding, marketing and digital media.
We specialise, we integrate and we deliver, using five sets
of skills - strategy, design, writing, production, and project
management.

We have enjoyed eight years of progressive growth. Now
we are the 10th largest independent creative agency in the
UK. Our clients include some of Britain's best brands. Last
year we won numerous effectiveness awards. We attract
and nurture some 60 of the industry's most talented people,
whose creative minds are dedicated to the needs of our
clients.

Clients
Virgin
BBC
Royal Mail
Hertz
Ordnance Survey
Interserve plc
Thetrainline
uSwitch
Land Registry
Nelsonbach
Transport for London
Department of Health
COI Communications
UK Trade & Investment
Fox Williams
Cisco Systems
Azzurri

**See also Branding and Graphic Design p. 86,
Packaging Design p. 144 and Interior, Retail and Event
Design p. 202**

1 thetrainline and thetrainlinestore websites
2 Virgin Atlantic Upper Class Suite microsite
3 Virgin Atlantic milesmorefriends microsite
4 Virgin Mobile interactive TV advertising campaign
5 Virgin Atlantic Upper Class Suite video
6 BBC World Service corporate video

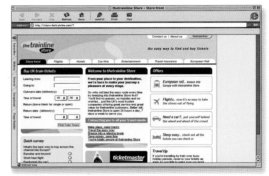

1

2

3

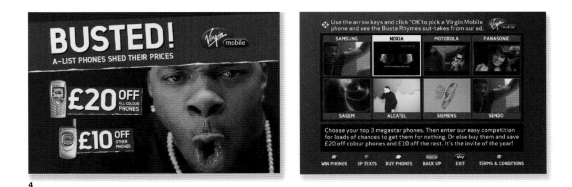

4

5

6

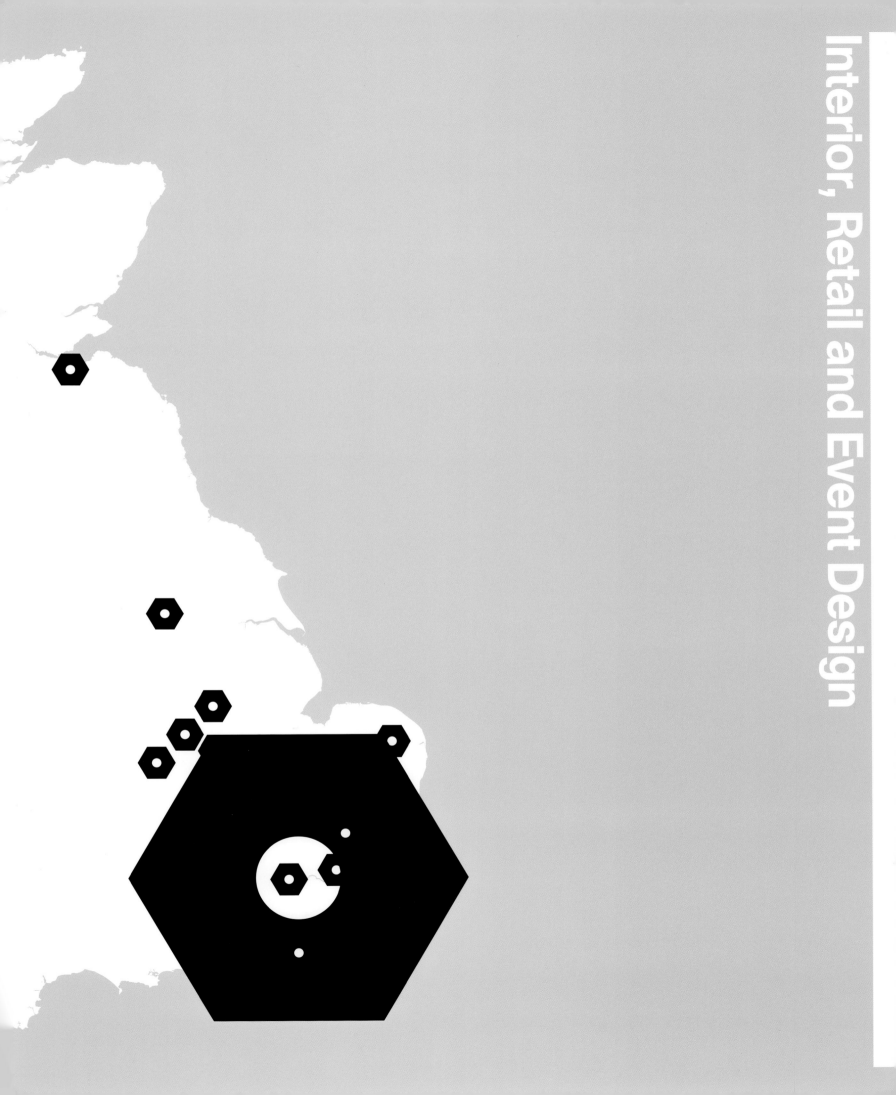

A.D. Creative Consultants

The Royal Victoria Patriotic Building / Trinity Road
London SW18 3SX
T +44 (0)20 8870 8743 / F +44 (0)20 8877 1151
hello@adcreative.co.uk
www.adcreative.co.uk

Contacts John Graham, Graham MacLeod, Gary Page
Staff 15 **Founded** 1973 **Memberships** Chartered Society
of Designers, Marketing Society, IOD, Design Council
registered

Company Profile
Highly experienced team with leading clients in major
national and international markets. Our work is on virtually
every high street in the UK today. We are also active in
countries as diverse as Saudi Arabia, Turkey and Italy.

We provide solutions that are suitably different, not just
simply different. With over 30 years of successful practice,
combined with proven ability and client references to back it
up, from food to fashion to fun to the outrageously famous...

Some of Our Friends
Marks & Spencer
Coca Cola
Playtopia
Dixons
PC World
The Link
Currys
Sainsburys
Big Yellow Storage Company
Henkel
Compass
Alize
Hartz (USA)
Disney

1 Playtopia Spaceworld UK, strategy, branding and
   graphics
2 Marks & Spencer, complete 24000 sq ft foods scheme
3 Marks & Spencer Marble Arch, complete store
   navigation scheme and graphics
4 Dixons, brand design and store badging
5 PC World, brand design and store badging
6 Big Yellow, graphics, retail and packaging

1

2

2

3

4

5

6

Aukett Limited

2 Great Eastern Wharf / Parkgate Road / London SW11 4TT
T +44 (0)20 7924 4949 / F +44 (0)20 7978 6720
Email@aukett.com
www.aukett.com

Company Profile
Aukett is an international group of Architects, Designers
and Engineers, with offices in London, Glasgow, Amsterdam,
Berlin, Dublin, Frankfurt, Milan, Prague and Warsaw.
The practice currently has 164 staff operating from its Head
Office in London and over 250 in offices across Europe.

Our design disciplines include Masterplanning, Architecture,
Structural Engineering, Services Engineering, Urban Design,
Landscape Architecture, Interior Design, Space Planning,
and Graphic Design.

We have developed a specialist expertise in Workplace
Design. This derives from a close involvement with our
clients in developing the brief and understanding their needs
in order to integrate working methods within an effective
space utilisation strategy. Our Workplace Consultancy
Service includes the following: Workplace Analysis; Brief
Development; Strategic Planning; Building Audits; Space
Budgets; Space Planning and New Working Environments.

Clients
Diageo
BT
RBS
Microsoft
BSkyB
Shell
Sun Microsystems
Procter & Gamble
Norwich Union
NATS

1   Presentation Pod
2   Internal walkway
3   Reception vinyl graphics (photo courtesy of Endpoint)
4   Bailey's Room
5   Gordon's Room

All photos: Diageo Headquarters, Park Royal

172

BDP Design

16 Brewhouse Yard / Clerkenwell / London EC1V 4LJ
T +44 (0)20 7812 8000 / F +44 (0)20 7812 8399
m-cook@bdp.co.uk
www.bdpdesign.co.uk

Management Martin Cook **Contact** Martin Cook
Staff 46 **Founded** 1972 **Memberships** Chartered Society of
Designers, Royal Society of Arts

Company Profile

BDP design is a multi-discipline design group with a wide
range of skills and expertise across both public and private
sectors. Our experience spans retail, leisure, education,
workplace, healthcare and transport design.

Our key strength lies in the integration of a wide range of
creative disciplines to provide creative services and
solutions across a diverse range of projects. Numerous
leading brands are represented by many of our clients, with
whom we have formed lasting relationships in both the UK
and throughout Europe.

We believe in bringing the best skills and experience
together to produce customer-focussed solutions.

Selected Clients

Nike
Marks & Spencer
B Sky B
Goldfish
Manchester United
Royal Bank of Scotland
Banco Santander
Rubicon Retail
Land Securities
Lend Lease
St George plc
City Academy, Bristol
BT Ignite

1   Corporate hospitality suite, Manchester United
2   Display lighting, Brighton Museum
3   Break-out space, Halifax headquarters
4   Prospectus, The City Academy, Bristol
5   Mosaic, Tres Aguas, Madrid
6   Restaurant, BDP Studios
7   Brand identity, The City Academy, Bristol
8   Interior branding, Goldfish, Glasgow
9   Restaurant screen, BT ignite

174

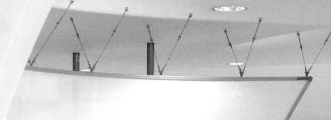

Learning COMES FIRST

Learning has the capacity to improve all
our lives and as such is at the heart of
all that we do. The City Academy,
Bristol is a learning community, a place
where we learn with and from one
another, where we recognise and
celebrate success and where we provide
the challenge and support needed for
high levels of achievement.

Learning about learning

Understanding how we learn is the key
to unlocking what we learn. As such we
help young people explore different
learning styles, discover new ways of
learning and become more effective and
successful learners.

04

The City Academy
BRISTOL

Learning comes first Learning about learning Learning to live together Learning today for tomorrow

Checkland Kindleysides Ltd

Charnwood Edge / Cossington / Leicester LE7 4UZ
Leicestershire
T +44 (0)116 2644 700 / F +44 (0)116 2644 701
marketing@checkind.com
www.checkind.com

Management Jeff Kindleysides, Principal Creative Director
Staff 85 **Founded** 1979

Company Profile
One of the largest independent design consultancies in the
UK and founded in 1979, we celebrate our 25th year in 2004.
We are a multi-disciplined design consultancy which
specialises in engaging consumers through graphic
communication, interiors and interactive design. We work in
partnership with both local and global brands on large and
small scale projects. 'Creative knowledge' best describes
our offer, as within our unique, purpose-built studios, we
have both the raw talent and inventive thinkers to design in
every discipline – along with the experience, knowledge and
understanding to physically deliver.

Expertise
Retail & Interiors
Graphics & Point of Sale
Brand & Corporate Identity
Packaging
Exhibitions
Web & Multimedia

Clients
Amtico
Bentley Motors
Boots
Design Council
George at ASDA
Hammonds
Henri-Lloyd
KFC
Kohler Mira
Levi Strauss®
Marks and Spencer
Minton
Principles
Ray-Ban
Rolls-Royce
Royal Doulton
Speedo
Thorntons
Vodafone

Awards
Design Agency of the Year 2003
Marketing Magazine

Retail Interiors Awards 2002
Best Small Shop Single Store - Cinch

ISP/VM&SD International Store Interior Design
Competition 2002
Cinch - Special Award for Merchandising Concept

Retail Week Award 2001
Store Design of the Year
Lunn Poly Holiday Superstore

DBA Design Effectiveness Award 2000
Retail & Leisure Category - Levi's® London Project

See also Branding and Graphic Design p. 32

Dalziel and Pow Design Consultants

5-8 Hardwick Street / London EC1R 4RG
T +44 (0)20 7837 7117 / F +44 (0)20 7837 7137
info@dalziel-pow.co.uk
www.dalziel-pow.co.uk

Management David Dalziel, Rosalyn Scott, Jackie Ware,
Keith Ware, Alastair Kean
Contacts David Dalziel, Rosalyn Scott
Staff 40 **Founded** 1983

Company Profile
Dalziel and Pow have developed a reputation founded on
effective design solutions for the retail market.

Through understanding the clients' brand, concepts are
designed to influence the market and achieve a dynamic
environment through interior, branding, packaging, art
direction and new media services.

Dalziel and Pow are founder members of All-Around-Design,
an association of independent European design consultants
sharing complementary skills and knowledge enabling each
member to deliver effective strategic design solutions to
brands reaching global and local markets.

Clients
Argos
Arnotts
Assa Abloy
BRE Multibank
Etam
Guinness UDV
Guta Bank
Hallmark
House of Fraser
Hugo Boss
Illum
...Instore
Jaeger
John Lewis
Jones Bootmaker
NCR
Nokia
Past Times
Penneys
Primark
River Island
Signet
Speedo
Stanfords
Tottenham Hotspur FC
Toyota
Unilever
World Duty Free Europe

1   Speedo Brand Store, Bondi
2   River Island, Flagship London
3   Nokia, global 3D branded environments

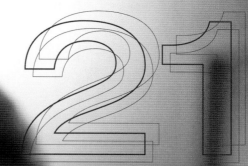

DALZIEL + POW

DALZIEL AND POW ARE CELEBRATING 21 YEARS OF DESIGN FOR THE RETAIL MARKET AND HAVE GROWN TO BECOME A MAJOR CONTRIBUTOR TO THE INCREASING REPUTATION OF DESIGN IN THE UK, and the global awareness of design as a positive force in the creation and development of retail brand identities. We believe firmly in the role of design to connect with consumers, making them feel good about your proposition, bringing financial and emotional rewards. We offer 100% commitment, an open and positive outlook with skilled designers bringing creativity and experience to any brief.

01

02

03

Design LSM

The Bath House / 58 Livingstone Road / Hove
Brighton BN3 3WL / East Sussex
T +44 (0)1273 820 033 / F +44 (0)1273 820 058
emily@designlsm.com
www.designlsm.com

Management Steve LaBouchardiere, Simon McCarthy,
David Rooney, Tim Burford **Contact** Emily Dent
Staff 11 **Founded** 1988

Company Profile
Our fully integrated design, architecture and turnkey
capabilities provide clients with a variety of comprehensive
services that combine creativity, knowledge and
commitment. By understanding current market influences
and the importance of a fresh, open-minded perspective,
designLSM provides the most effective solution.

Services
Interior Design
Graphic Design
Architecture
Quantity Surveying

Clients
Apartment 195
Apostrophe
Amano
Carluccio's
Debenhams
Eagle Bar Diner
Funky Buddha
Hilton Group
Lacoste
Pied a Terre
The Real Eating Company
Spur

1   Eagle Bar Diner, London
2   Lacoste, Knightsbridge
3   Carluccio's, West Smithfield
4   Funky Buddha Nightclub, London
5   Debenhams, Bullring Birmingham
6   Apostrophe, London
7   Apartment 195, London
8   Forest Hotel, Dorridge
9   Ebony Bar, Brighton

180

1

9

8

2

3

4

7

6

5

Enterprise IG
The Global Brand Design Agency

11-33 St John Street / London EC1M 4PJ
T +44 (0)20 7559 7000 / F +44 (0)20 7559 7001
enquiries@enterpriseig.com
www.enterpriseig.co.uk

Contact Ms Robin Kadrnka, Group Marketing Director
Founded 1976

We've been around for over 25 years and are the world's leading global brand design agency, employing some 650 people in 24 offices worldwide. Part of the WPP Group, Enterprise IG works with global product suppliers and service providers to bring their brands to life through retail and leisure experiences, live events, sponsorship programmes and interactive media.

Our focus on consumer insights enables us to predict the changing needs and aspirations of consumers, on both a global and local level. This ensures the solutions we deliver for our clients are totally relevant within a fluid marketplace.

Our brand experience programmes have delivered business growth for clients such as Vodafone, Unilever, Nike, Alliance & Leicester, SONY, Audi, Dockers, Waterstone's, Whitbread, Ministry of Sound, John Lewis and Siemens.

See also Branding and Graphic Design p. 38 and Packaging Design p. 120

1 Vodafone
2 Lipton
3 Waterstone's
4 Audi Forum

3

4

Fitch

121-141 Westbourne Terrace / London W2 6JR
T +44 (0)20 7479 0900 / F +44 (0)20 7479 0600
agoodall@fitchlondon.com
www.fitch.com

Management Rodney Fitch, Scott Wolfe (worldwide),
Lucy Unger, Tim Greenhalgh (London)
Contacts Ashley Goodall (London), Caroline O'Driscoll
(worldwide), Richard McHardy (Pci:Live)
+44 (0)20 7544 7500
Staff 70 **Founded** 1972 **Memberships** D&AD, ISTD,
CSD, DBA

Company Profile
Fitch is a consumer-driven design company. It was
founded in 1972 by Rodney Fitch, in the belief that social
improvement and business success are not incompatible,
and that design is the bridge that connects the two.

Fitch offers four core areas of expertise. A comprehensive
retail capability – from retail developments, shops, stores
and restaurants to in-store merchandising, implementation
and procurement; product development and invention
strategies; brand communications including identities,
in-store and environmental graphics, packaging and live
events; and lastly, trends forecasting.

Fitch services local, regional and global clients through
a global studio of 500 people based at 19 locations
in 13 countries in Asia Pacific, Europe, the Middle East
and North America.

We believe that as companies, markets and technologies
grow ever more complex, our core message of simple
and dynamic human engagement with the material world
through good design remains true. Fitch continues to create
distinctive, authentic experiences through a deep
understanding of and responsiveness to, consumer needs,
wants and desires.

Clients Include
Aquascutum
Asian Games 2006
BAT
Ben & Jerry's
Bentley Motors
BP
Cadbury Adams
Federated Department Stores
General Motors
LEGO
Microsoft
Nissan
Panasonic
Proton
Toys'R'Us
Vodafone
Yum!Brands

01

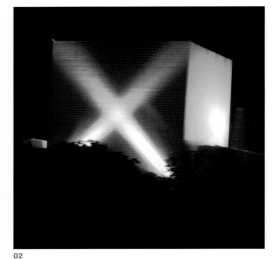

02

03

04

05

06

01,02 Microsoft Xbox
Live event design and production
to communicate Microsoft's vision
and long-term goals for Xbox to
an international press audience
(Prelive)

03,04 BAT 35° F
Concept creation and interior design
for a 'chill out' bar in Geneva, for
BAT's Lucky Strike brand

05,06,07 LEGO
Retail brand strategy and design
for LEGO stores worldwide
to communicate LEGO'S core
philosophy of 'play well'

IDa
Interior Design Associates

Studio 5 Moira Furnace / Moira / Derbyshire DE12 6AT
T +44 (0)1283 229 998 / F +44 (0)1283 229 909
studio@idadesign.co.uk
www.idadesign.co.uk

Management Gareth Humphreys, Sarah Rankine
Staff 7 **Founded** 2000 **Membership** RIBA

Company Profile
IDa is a versatile team of Interior Designers, Architects and Project Managers who have expertise in many areas of interior architecture.

The majority of our work has been in the hospitality, leisure and retail sectors where innovation and new concepts have been developed.

We believe in working closely with our clients in order to develop highly effective solutions which are also operationally practical, placing great emphasis that all projects, large or small, are on time and on budget.

Our ability to deliver is further enhanced by our experience, knowledge and understanding of planning issues, building regulations, statutory approvals, contract administration and a hands-on approach to site works to see the projects to completion.

1 Tin Tin – Leeds
2 Thai Edge – Cardiff
3 Thai Edge – Leeds
4 Waterhead Hotel Reception – Ambleside
5 Del Villaggio – Birmingham
6 Del Villaggio – Birmingham
7 Del Villaggio – Birmingham
8 Waterhead Hotel Restaurant – Ambleside
9 Waterhead Hotel Bedroom – Ambleside
10 Waterhead Hotel Restaurant – Ambleside

1

2

3

4

5

6

7

8

9

Landesign

7 Blake Mews / Kew / Richmond-upon-Thames TW9 3QA
T +44 (0)20 8332 6699 / F +44 (0)20 8332 6095
info@landdesignstudio.co.uk
www.landdesignstudio.co.uk

Management Peter Higgins, James Dibble, Shirley Walker
Contact Peter Higgins
Staff 12 **Founded** 1992 **Membership** RIBA

Company Profile

We have always had a simple ambition – to create
the type of consultancy that would encourage creative
and systematic design solutions, acknowledging the real
needs of our clients.

Landesign's involvement with clients is increasingly
at a strategic level, where we are able to provide support
in the early stages of the business plan and marketing
development initiatives. Our design skills provide a point
of difference when considering the function of the brand
in the marketplace.

This is best demonstrated by the Famous Grouse
Experience that opened in June 2002 at the Glenturret
Distillery (Scotland), which involves an architectural pavilion,
extensive interpretation and an immersive, interactive
environment. In 2002 it received the BAFTA Interactive
Award in the Sport and Leisure category, and in 2003,
the Marketing Brand Design Award (Best in Show).

Landesign's most innovative project has been the PlayZone
at The Millennium Dome – which was voted 'Best Zone'
by an ICM Poll, Holiday Which Magazine and The Times.
It also won the FX International Interior Design Award for
Best Entertainment Venue in 2000. As a result of this
experience, we are continuing to research and develop
the potential of digital interactivity.

In response to the complexity of the ever-evolving cultural
industries, Landesign are currently collaborating with
Central St. Martins College of Art & Design (London) in the
development of an MA course entitled 'Creative Practice in
Narrative Environments'.

Clients

Ars Electronica
BBC
British Film Institute
Ford Motor Company
Foreign & Commonwealth Office (UK)
Greenpeace
Highland Distillers Ltd.
Isle of Man Government
Imperial War Museum (London)
Museum of Science & Industry in Manchester
National Maritime Museum (Cornwall & Greenwich)
National Museums & Galleries Wales
Natural History Museum (London)
NESTA
Province of I-Lan (Taiwan)
River & Rowing Museum (Henley)
Royal Botanic Gardens (Kew)
The National Football Museum (Preston)
The Science Museum (London)

1-3 CableTel Mobile, UK, 1996
4   Moving Objects, Royal College of Art, UK, 1998
5-6 PlayZone, Millennium Dome, UK, 2000
7   Dinobirds, Natural History Museum, UK, 2001
8   Futures, Thinktank, UK, 2001
9   Imagining the City, Urbis, Manchester, UK, 2002
10   National Maritime Museum Cornwall, UK, 2003
11   The Famous Grouse Experience, Crieff, UK, 2002

1

2

4

6

7

10

3

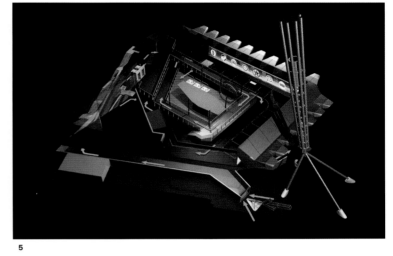

5

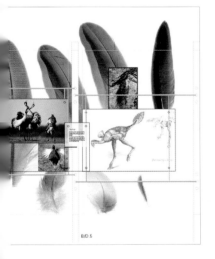

B/D.5

8

9

11

Mansfields
Connecting brands to the real world

Bentalls / Pipps Hill Industrial Estate / Basildon SS14 3BX
Essex
T +44 (0)1268 520646 / F +44 (0)1268 526865
mike@mansfieldsdesign.co.uk
www.mansfieldsdesign.co.uk

Management Andy Frankland, Ivor Frankland, Don Jones,
Peter Kay **Contact** Mike Hayward
Staff 19 **Founded** 1905 **Memberships** ISO 9002, ISO 14001,
Institute of Directors

Company Profile
Mansfields is a marketing services agency, specialising
in the creation, design and implementation of live events,
exhibitions, graphics media, digital media and film media.

We advise our clients on how to target an audience and then
produce a live event solution, design solution or media
solution to fulfil the client's objectives. Our style of working
is consensual, better described as working in partnership
with our clients, although we take full responsibility for
projects and programmes under our care, often working in
a way that looks as if we are the client's own internal team.

By enabling organisations to communicate effectively
to key internal and external audiences, we can contribute
successfully to such wide-ranging initiatives as brand,
service and product launches, internal communications
programmes, media briefing projects, shareholder
meetings, business events and consumer events.

Clients
Crawford
Dynix
Ford
FM Global
Hanover International
Jaguar
Moss Bros
Thorn
WJB Chiltern

1   Ford Focus C-Max launch event
2   Thorn exhibition
3   Jaguar X-Type Estate launch event
4   Jaguar XJ Long Wheelbase Press Pack
5   Thorn video
6   Visos media information
7   Ingeni multimedia Compact Disc
8   Technical video
9   Retail Environment design
10 Moss Bros exhibition design

Connecting brands to the real world

3D design

Multimedia

Film & Video

Graphic design

Project Management

Live communications

breathe fresh air ↗

MoreySmith

24 Marshalsea Road / London SE1 1HF
T + 44 (0)20 7089 1470 / F + 44 (0)20 7378 1274
information@morey.co.uk
www.moreysmith.com

Management Linda Morey Smith, Andrew McCann,
Simon Flint
Staff 20 **Founded** 1993 **Memberships** British Council
for Offices, Design Business Association, Chartered Society
of Designers

Company Profile

MoreySmith is a multi-disciplinary consultancy, practising
a 'total design' that eloquently expresses a client's individual
character and accurately solves its functional and
operational problems. Both, if humanly possible, under
budget and ahead of schedule.

This unique personality and personal approach does not
mean that a 'house style' is imposed on a project. Far from it.
A professional consultancy listens to and learns a client
company's needs, then develops the ideas and the
programme exactly appropriate to the individual brief and
budget. MoreySmith's design serves your agenda, not its
own.

Clients

AstraZeneca
Channel Four
Electronic Arts
EMI
Mayer Brown Rowe & Maw
MCI
Merck, Sharpe & Dohme
Microsoft
Royal Commonwealth Society
Sony Music
Sport England
Warner Bros
Yahoo

1 Sport England, media meeting area
2 Sport England, reception area
3 Mayer Brown Rowe & Maw, reception area
4 Mayer Brown Rowe & Maw, foyer
5 EMI Headquarters, atrium
6 EMI Headquarters, boardroom
7 EMI Headquarters, atrium
8 EMI Headquarters, working environment
9 EMI Headquarters, stairs
10 EMI Headquarters, reception area

1

2

3

4

5

6

7

8

9

10

Navyblue Design Group

122 Giles Street / Edinburgh EH6 6BZ
T +44 (0)131 553 5050 / F +44 (0)131 555 0707
edinburgh@navyblue.com
www.navyblue.com

Third Floor Morelands / 17-21 Old Street
London EC1V 9HL
T +44 (0)20 7253 0316 / F +44 (0)20 7553 9409
london@navyblue.com
www.navyblue.com

Management Douglas Alexander, Managing Director
Navyblue Scotland, Geoff Nicol, Managing Director
Navyblue London
Contacts Mike Lynch, Business Development Director,
Toby Southgate, Client Services Director
Staff 68 **Founded** 1994

Company Profile
Navyblue's core business is creative design and
communications, supported by internal strategic planning
and research – one of our values is "thinking out louder™",
and this approach influences everything we do. Since 1994
we have expanded our skill-set from traditional graphics into
the areas of 3d environments and new media, incorporating
technical development expertise as well as on-screen
design capability. Navyblue is one of the UK's top 30 design
consultancies, employing more than 65 people and with
a turnover in excess of £7 million.

Retail, Interior and Event Design
Navyblue 3d design specialises in the design and creation
of retail interiors, exhibitions, commercial environments
and visitor centres – the entire spectrum of 3d brand
expression. As with all Navyblue projects, thinking is a
critical part of the process. Our creative solutions are
always the result of a clear understanding of clients'
business objectives, an appreciation of their culture,
and considerable thought and planning.

Clients
Ahlstrom – exhibitions programme, bespoke stands,
Europe and US
Carrick Jewellery – Catherine Shaw brand creation and
shop environments
Drambuie – exhibition stands and promotional bar units
Food Standard Agency – UK exhibitions programme
Frankfurt Development Agency – exhibitions, Europe
Intelligent Finance – exhibitions
Michael Laing Jewellery – retail environments
Orange – trade and consumer exhibitions programme,
UK and Europe
Royal Bank of Scotland – exhibitions and office promotional
display units
Scottish Equitable – exhibitions

See also Branding and Graphic Design p. 64, Packaging
Design p. 130 and New Media Design p. 160

1   Orange TMA Trade Show exhibition
2   Orange TMA Trade Show exhibition
3   The Scotland Stand MIPM Trade Show
4   EDI MIPM Trade Show
5   Frankfurt Economic Development Agency MIPM
    Trade Show

1

3

4

2

5

The Nest

200 St John Street / London EC1V 4RN
T +44 (0)20 7689 8344 / F +44 (0)20 7689 8347
info@thenest.co.uk
www.thenest.co.uk

Company Profile

The Nest specialises in helping brands connect with people in a positive emotional way.

Experience has taught us that the most effective brands possess a strong sense of humanity. We make it our business to deliver this for our clients, working organically across branding, strategy, interiors, communications and product design.

In each of the four projects showcased here, we worked with a huge variety of people in order to ensure that our work matched up to customer expectations and needs. To re-invent WHSmith, we collaborated with their innovation team on a daily basis, constantly editing stock lines and reviewing adjacencies to create dramatically different customer flows – and similarly striking sales. At the Eden Project, we worked alike with local schoolchildren and experts in sustainability; with herbalists at Neal's Yard Remedies; and with conservation experts, education officers and curators at the British Library.

We hope you like the results as much as we do.

Clients

British Airways
British Library
Cadbury
Eden Project
Kurt Geiger
MFI
Neal's Yard Remedies
Old Vic
PizzaExpress
Rip Curl
Ryness
Salvation Army
Selfridges
Sofa Workshop
WHSmith

1-2 WHSmith concept store, Guildford
3 Indigo Café, The Eden Project, Cornwall
4 Neal's Yard Remedies, London
5 'The Silk Road' exhibition, British Library, London

196

1

2

3

4

5

Pocknell Studio

Readings / Blackmore End / Braintree / Essex / CM7 4DH
T +44 (0)1787 463 206 / F +44 (0)1787 462 122
andrea@pocknellstudio.com
www.pocknellstudio.com

Contacts Andrea Green, Will Pocknell
Staff 10 **Memberships** STD, CSD, D&AD

Company Profile
Pocknell Studio is a retail, environmental and graphic design
practice established over 20 years. Retail design, involving
brand identity, store design, packaging and point of sale,
is a strong part of the studio's competence, as is the design
of corporate identity, communications and environments.
Clients include businesses in the automotive, leisure, food,
pharmaceutical, research, publishing and transport sectors.
Pocknell Studio takes care to understand its clients and their
needs and as a result enjoys many long-term business
relationships.

Pocknell works on large and small projects around the world
and has won several design awards in its various disciplines.

Clients
Crabtree & Evelyn (Overseas) Ltd
Seattle Coffee Company
London Transport
4D Berhard Malaysia
Oi! Bagel
Fresh Italy
Planet Organic
Greene King plc
English Heritage
Soup Opera
Plant Vegetarian
Tomos Watkin & Sons
Evan Evans Brewery
Maxelreiner Breweries
Vysoky Chlumec Brewery
The Food Company
Fresh 'n' Smooth
Macaw (Soft Drinks) Ltd
Santa Fe
Rapallo

"The most important thing about selecting Pocknell Studio was that they really wanted to do it. They really liked the concept and were brimming with ideas from the beginning"

Tom Allchurch *Fresh Italy*
Design Week, May 2004

Best price for a retail coffee chain. "Acquired by Starbucks for £52m"

Telegraph Money

"London's best bagel shops"

Time Out

"Best Supermarket and Food Retailing Winner"

Retail Interiors Award

"[Plant] is set to revitalise the weary eco-heavy image of vegetarianism"

Wallpaper*

"Best Newcomer Finalist"

Retailers Retailer Award

★★★★★

Pocknell

Reinvigorate
Brand Consultants

2 Gads Hill / Trimmingham Road / Halifax
West Yorkshire HX2 7PX
T +44 (0)1422 340 055 / F +44 (0)1422 340 055
martin@reinvigorate.co.uk
www.reinvigorate.co.uk

Contact Martin Monks
Staff 3 + 27 specialists **Founded** 2003

Company Profile
Born out a desire to offer simple, honest, design that
delivers commercial results. A 'novel business model' where
the needs of a project are perfectly married with a team of
specialists; to deliver on-time and in budget. Fact not hype.
Passion and imagination without the bull****!

Expertise
Retail Interiors
Graphics & Point of Sale
Brand & Corporate Identity
Web & Multimedia

Clients
Adams Childrenswear
Boots plc
Calderdale College
English Heritage
Go Outdoors
Hallmark Cards

1 Adams Childrenswear – Energise Store
2 Boots – mini mode concession
3 Calderdale College – Identity & Signage
4 Hallmark - Marks & Spencers – Lifestore

revitalise

refresh

recreate

refurb

reaction

refine

reform

reunite

reliable

restore

Start Creative Limited

2 Sheraton Street / Soho / London W1F 8BH
T +44 (0)20 7269 0101 / F +44 (0)20 7269 0102
jen@startcreative.co.uk
startcreative.co.uk

Management Mike Curtis, Darren Whittingham,
Jennifer McAleer, Ian Kempen **Contact** Jennifer McAleer
Staff 59 **Founded** 1996

Company Profile
We're in the business of ideas and creativity. Here, we think
differently and this makes Start an exciting place to be.

Start is a creative agency with one aim – to deliver inspiring
creativity to meet business needs. We have burning passion
for three things – branding, marketing and digital media.
We specialise, we integrate and we deliver, using five sets
of skills – strategy, design, writing, production, and project
management.

We have enjoyed eight years of progressive growth. Now
we are the 10th largest independent creative agency in the
UK. Our clients include some of Britain's best brands. Last
year we won numerous effectiveness awards. We attract
and nurture some 60 of the industry's most talented people,
whose creative minds are dedicated to the needs of our
clients.

Clients
Virgin
BBC
Royal Mail
Hertz
Ordnance Survey
Interserve plc
Thetrainline
uSwitch
Land Registry
Nelsonbach
Transport for London
Department of Health
COI Communications
UK Trade & Investment
Fox Williams
Cisco Systems
Azzurri

**See also Branding and Graphic Design p. 86,
Packaging Design p. 144 and New Media Design p. 166**

1 Virgin Mobile concession store
2 Virgin Mobile catalogue
3 Virgin Mobile packaging
4 Virgin Mobile 'celebrity' catalogue with online promotion

2

3

1

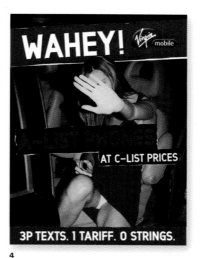

4

Tibbatts Associates Ltd
Design Consultants & Architects

1 St Pauls Square / Birmingham B3 1QU / West Midlands
T +44 (0)121 236 9000 / F +44 (0)121 236 8705
info@tibbatts.co.uk
www.tibbatts.com

Management Neil Tibbatts **Contact** Carmel Watts
Founded 1979

Company Profile

Tibbatts Associates' team was established in 1979 and has for the past 25 years specialised in servicing the Leisure Hospitality Hotel and Entertainment industry.

The firm's track record is long established, with considerable breadth of activity in projects ranging from the one-off small independent restaurant to the £100M+ holiday village development, covering hotel, bar, cinema, theatre, casino, F&B, fine dining, health & fitness, spa, and all stops between.

Whilst the bulk of Tibbatts Associates' work is in the U.K., the firm has designed venues in the Far and Middle East, Europe, Africa and North America, collaborating with consultants, clients, suppliers and contractors worldwide.

Tibbatts' professional team comprises a blend of designers, architects and technicians with project planning and management support, ensuring that projects are creatively conceived and technically executed to a proper time and cost discipline.

Tibbatts Associates' long and specialised experience means that they can talk the same language as Leisure and Hospitality operators and deliver environmental solutions that not only generate customer interest, but are practically operable and serviceable in order to achieve the commercial objectives of its clients.

For further information and copies of our update booklet mailing, please email info@tibbatts.co.uk.

Watt
Strategic Brand Specialists

Watt UK / Ring Road / West Park / Leeds LS16 6RA
T +44 (0)113 288 3210 / F +44 (0)113 275 6044
info@whatswatt.co.uk
www.whatswatt.co.uk

Watt International / 172 John Street
Toronto / Ontario / Canada M5T 1X5
T +1 416 593 7254 / F +1 416 593 7940
contactus@wattinternational.com
www.wattinternational.com

Company Profile
We are straight-talking, hard-hitting brand specialists.

From environmental design to complete brand architecture, we have the capabilities and expertise to deliver profitable business and design solutions.

See also Packaging Design p. 148

1 Oxford Properties, Toronto, Canada
2 Hotworx, Texas, USA
3 Paramount, Famous Players, Toronto, Canada
4 La Maison Simons, Québec, Canada
5 Sportchek, The Forzani Group, Canada
6 Armstrong, North America

Philip Watts Design

32b Shakespere Street / Nottingham NG5 2HE
Nottinghamshire
T +44 (0)115 947 4809 / F +44 (0)115 947 5828
sales@philipwattsdesign.com
www.philipwattsdesign.com

Management Philip Watts **Contact** Philip Watts
Staff 10 **Founded** 1994

Company Profile
Formed in 1994, Philip Watts Design has continually grown both in size and creativity.

Our highly successful creative architectural ironmongery range – spearheaded by the innovative portholes for doors kits – has helped to form a family of over 60 products regularly specified for both national and international products by some of the most respected architects currently working.

This design-and-build mentality has helped to push the interior side of the business forward with increasingly challenging projects and installations.

Our strengths rest in developing full concepts, from name generation through to the opening night; we work closely with our clients and are flexible enough to accept unforeseen deviations and changes to original specifications.

The Philip Watts Design style is usually signified by a subtle blend of creativity, experience and irreverence. This can be found in any of our projects, from melting aluminium staircases to Alsace influenced bar concepts.

Clients
British Airways
Virgin
BBC
Channel 4
LWT
Heathrow Airport
Burger King
McDonalds
Costa Coffee
Disneyland Paris
Conran
Gillette
Seymore Powell

1-7   4550 Miles From Delhi contemporary Indian restaurant, Nottingham, independant leisure, 2002
8-13   Sausage Bar, Nottingham, Ever1956, 2004
14   Stainless steel porthole with integral pull bar, in-house product range, 2002
15   Stainless steel lozenge porthole kits, in-house product range, 2001
16   Amorphous staircase, Les Houches, France, private client, 2001
17-19   Kingly Club members bar, Soho, London, Richmond Developments, 2003

208

6

7

12

13

17

18

19

cl design
creative design innovation

21 Main Road / Underwood / Nottinghamshire NG16 5GP
T +44 (0)1773 530 355 / F +44 (0)1773 533 823
info@cldesignltd.com
www.cldesignltd.com

Contacts Neil White, Steve Wagstaff

Company Profile
Cl design, formed in 1984, has consistently been at the
forefront of the design industry.

The services offered by cl design have been continually
expanded, with all clients benefiting from the complete
design process available in house. We have a dedicated
team of creative, multi-disciplinary designers creating
innovative, contemporary designs, all with built-in
manufacturability. Ours is a proven ability to work from
initial concept through to implementation, maintaining the
desired aesthetics of the product.

Our team of designers will create a balance of elegant
styling with ease of manufacture, encompassing all aspects
of your design brief. We believe in creating a relationship
between the design object and the user. Liasing closely with
you – the client – our team ensures that your key corporate
features are fully integrated into the design.

1 Brite Box, light therapy unit for (S.A.D.) sufferers
2 Tomy, activity sounds flower nursery toy
3 Newteam, NT1500 power shower
4 Arena seating, demountable folding stadia seating
5 Winsor and Newton, artists' paint pallet
6 Barnett International, revolution crossbow
7 Personna International, Tri-Flexx ladies system handle
8 Agi Media, Star Trek Voyager DVD packaging
9 MV Sports, Scoop-the-Digger sit and ride toy

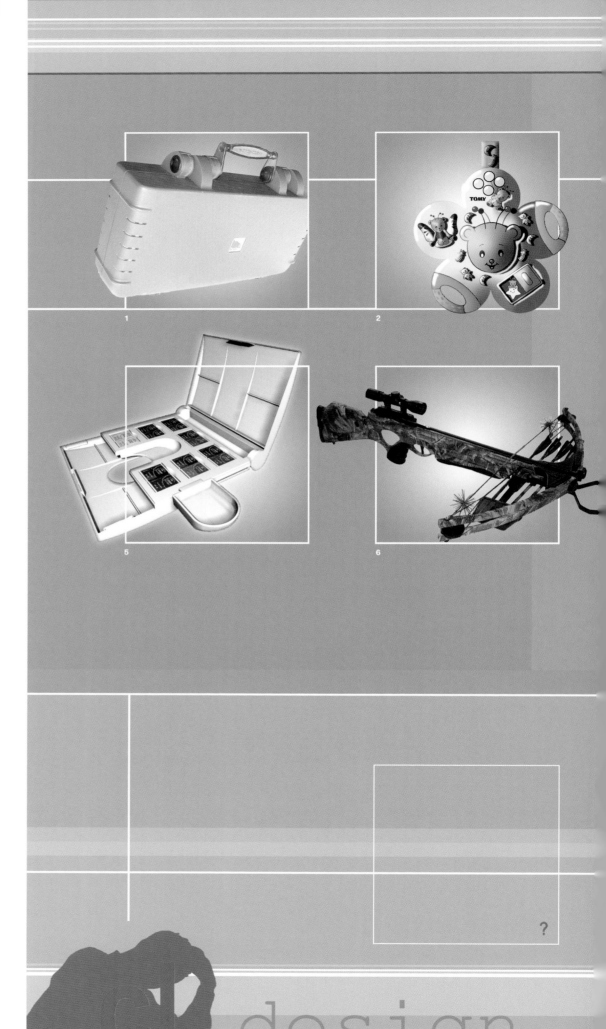

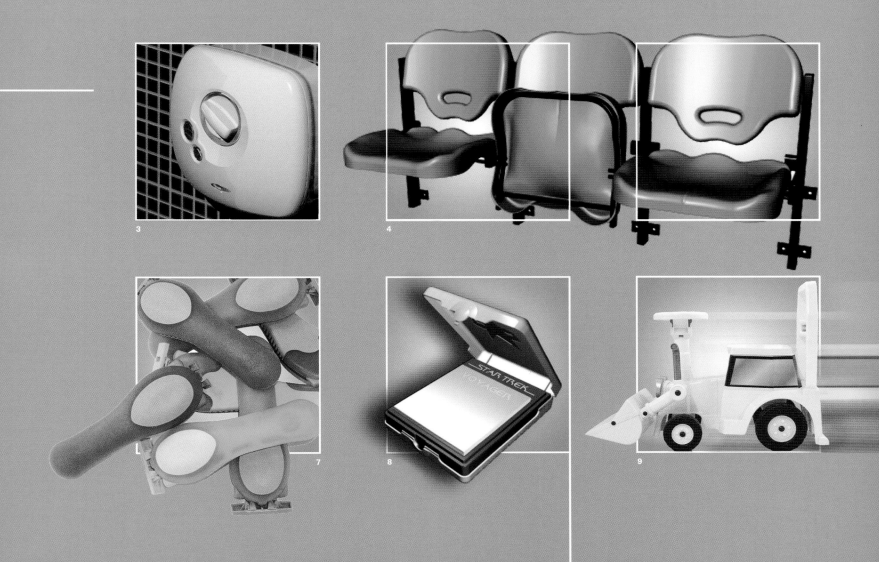

- creative conceptual vision
- product design innovation
- industrial design and engineering
- prototypes and styling models
- injection mould tool design
- corporate identity and branding
- project planning and management

Hothouse Product Development Partners

Unit 1 College Fields Business Centre
Prince George's Road / London SW19 2PT
T +44 (0)20 8687 2093 / F +44 (0)20 8646 1822
studio@hothouse-design.com
www.hothouse-design.com

Management Neville Pryke, Richard Thom, Peter Bessey
Contact Neville Pryke
Founded 1989 **Membership** Design Business Association
(DBA)

Hothouse is a consultancy specialising in innovation,
product design and development.
Design research: new ideas, conceptual and innovation
proposals
Design development: product design, image, use and
function
Technical development: prototyping for volume manufacture
Delivery: proven development process from start to finish
We aim to produce solutions that exceed expectation.

1 Radiotherapy Machine
  Hothouse won a 2003 Design Business Association
  (DBA) Design Effectiveness Award with its design of
  a patient-friendly new look for a high-precision
  radiotherapy unit. The award, given for the entire
  paneling and user interface design of Elekta Synergy™,
  recognised increased sales and the use of colour and
  ergonomics. Elekta 2003.
2 Ear Plug Dispenser
  For Aearo, Hothouse has designed new equipment for
  dispensing earplugs, which is both reliable and easy to
  use. The patented dispenser is environment friendly,
  reducing the need for excessive packaging, and has
  been installed in several factories, including major car
  manufacturers Ferrari, Audi and Nissan. Aearo 2000.
3 Self-service ticket vending machines
  Hothouse has teamed up with Ascom Transport Revenue
  to provide railway stations with a new customer-friendly
  range of ticketing machines. The machines, which are
  already being used at several stations, including Gatwick,
  Marylebone and Wokingham, meet new UK requirements
  for the disabled. Ascom 2003.
4 Boating Bullseye
  Hothouse has reinvented the yachting essential, the
  bullseye rope-control guide, which had previously
  remained unchanged for 50 years. The sleek, new
  Spinlock Bullseye can be attached to the boat deck in
  one easy fixing, enabling boat builders and DIY sailors
  to fix the device in half the time needed for traditional
  types. Spinlock 2002.
5 Filtered Water Pitcher
  The water pitcher has been designed by Hothouse to
  establish a strong product design equity for the PUR
  brand, suited to the kitchen and now the dining room as
  well. The elegant and differentiating shape is the result
  of reference to classic designs and innovative thinking,
  challenging and changing how the product is made –
  literally turning the original upside down!
  Procter & Gamble/PUR 2001.

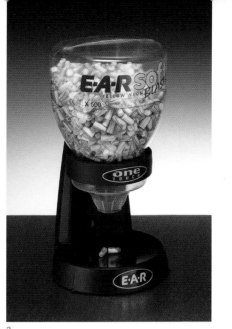

2

3

4

5

dba

Design Effectiveness
Award Winner 2003

1

David Morgan Associates

10 Broadbent Close / 20 - 22 Highgate High Street
London N6 5JW
T +44 (0)20 8340 4009 / F +44 (0)20 8348 6478
david@dmadesign.co.uk
www.dmadesign.co.uk

Contact David Morgan
Staff 5 **Founded** 1981 **Memberships** CSD, DBA

Better Design for Better Business
David Morgan Associates has designed successful new
products for clients around the world for over 20 years.

We specialise in the design of luminaires & lighting systems,
consumer and industrial products.

DMA handles the complete design and development
process, undertaking both consumer and technical
research, providing unique creative design solutions and
offering a comprehensive engineering, sourcing, testing
and project management service.

We produce work that works, which is why DMA's clients
return time and time again.

If you feel that better product design can improve the
performance of your business, contact us now.

Clients
A&M Records
Belfer Lighting
Biobrite
Boots
Cooper Lighting
Creation Records
Daiko Electric
Designplan
Kreon
L'Image Home Products
Louis Poulsen
Panasonic (Matsushita Electric Works)
Philips Lighting
Sony Europe
Thermax
Thorn Lighting

1   Panasonic Japan, Burlington desk light
2   Panasonic Japan, PAR Spotlight series
3   Sony Europe, Special edition CD Case
4   Thermax Vacuum Jug
5   Louis Poulsen SPR 12 Projector
6   Louis Poulsen SPR 14 Projector fresnel lens
7   Louis Poulsen SPR 14 Projector
8   Louis Poulsen Morph Spotlight

Panasonic Japan

Panasonic Japan

Sony Europe   Thermax

DAVID MORGAN ASSOCIATES

Louis Poulsen
Exterior lighting
SPR 12, SPR 14, Morph

PDD
The Innovation Partner

85-87 Richford Street / London W6 7HJ
T +44 (0)20 8735 1111 / F +44 (0)20 8735 1133
info@pdd.co.uk
www.pdd.co.uk

Management Helen Gray **Contact** Lara Hawketts
Staff 80 **Founded** 1978
Memberships RCA, CSD, D&AD, IDSA
Recent design awards D&AD, IDSA, Red Dot

"Number one product design consultancy 2003"
Design Week Creative League Survey – Top 100 Design
Groups

PDD specialises in product innovation.

This gives you access to a new type of innovation partner
where human insight, creativity and technical knowledge are
fused in a single process to deliver outstanding solutions.
Our vibrant, inventive culture focuses on the full new-
product cycle, from strategic research and visioning,
through detailed design, to complete engineered products
ready for manufacture and launch.

Our cross-functional teams are supported by leading-edge,
in-house facilities, including focus group suites, CAD-CAE,
prototyping and testing laboratory.

PDD is passionate about the intelligent cross-fertilisation
of experience and knowledge. The diversity of our business
combines with our collaborative teamwork to spark ideas
that lead to real business gains.

As companies seek to sustain their new product pipeline,
build their brands and enhance their agility, PDD offers a
responsive partnership to achieve more, faster.

218

Product Resolutions Ltd

The Royal / 25 Bank Plain / Norwich NR2 4SF
T +44 (0)1603 762 676 / F +44 (0)1603 762 656
design@productresolutions.com
www.productresolutions.com

Management Paul Robbins **Contacts** Paul Robbins,
Nick Harvey
Staff 6 **Founded** 2000 **Membership** BDI

Company Profile
Product Resolutions is a company with a fresh approach to
creating new products.

We offer a complete solution of innovation, design,
manufacture and supply. Working with you to maximise
commercial opportunities, we use our award-winning design
team and vast manufacturing experience to develop highly
creative and competitive new products.

Our clients range from inventors to multinational companies
in Europe, Asia and North America.

Services
Product design and development
New concept product generation
3D CAD visualisation
Mechanical design
Prototype and model making
Tooling supply and liaison
Manufacturing and supply from the Far East
Graphic design and packaging

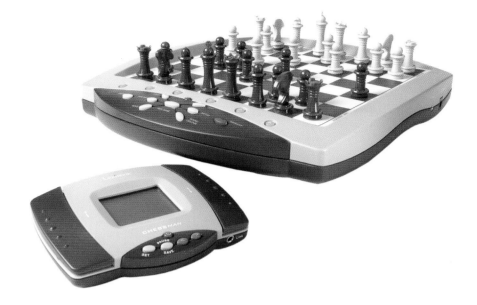

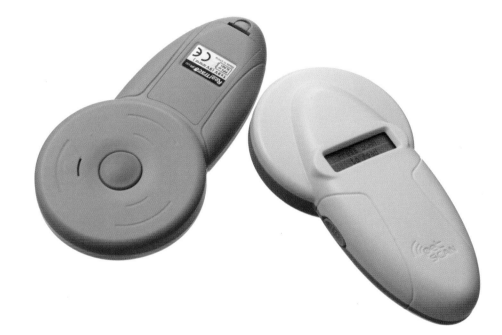

LUMIE

Tin Horse

Pelham House, Pelham Court / London Road
Marlborough SN8 2AG / Wiltshire
T +44 (0)1672 519 999 / F +44 (0)1672 511 811
info@tinhorse.com
www.tinhorse.com

Management Martin Bunce, John Lamb, Peter Booth
Contact Peter Booth
Staff 12 **Founded** 1990

One Can...
... use a single image to talk about what we do, because
our approach is fundamentally rooted in every project we
undertake. Tin Horse is a diverse team of creative thinkers
and designers with a few ambitions in common: we refuse
to accept banality, we are not limited by what is already out
there, we are prepared to challenge what is taken for
granted and finally, we have really big dreams for everyday
things.

Formed in 1990, we are structural design experts and our
core business is working on FMCG brands where we aim
to provide a seamless process which takes creative thought
into manufacturing reality.

Easy Can...
... made for painting. Our Deepsearch©* process revealed
that for more than 40 years, metal cans have ignored the
greatest causes of consumer frustration and difficulty with
trim painting: tools needed to open lids, messy in use, hard
to re-close and tiring to hold.

Tin Horse's 'easy can' for ICI Paints has revolutionised
the paint category through a paradigm shifting use of PET.
The pack has a screw cap, brush wipe, brush rest and easy
grip body. Not to mention a printed shrink sleeve that allows
you to see the actual colour of the paint inside.

They Can...
(Astra Zeneca, Boots Healthcare International, BP, Clinical
Designs Limited, Coca Cola, Colgate Palmolive, Compass
Maps, Coors, Diageo, Electrolux, Heinz, ICI, Kimberly Clark,
Lever Fabergé, Kraft Foods, P&G, Polycell, Unilever,
Uniq Foods)

... all tell you something about our work: the packs we've
created, the brands we've influenced and what it's like to
work with Tin Horse.

You Can...
... find out more about us, our work and our 'Can do'
approach to brands and innovation by calling Pete Booth.

*DeepSearch© is a bespoke Tin Horse / Consumer-interactive
design step, tailored to suit each project.

222

DOUBLE YOU

A COLLECTION BY HANNES WETTSTEIN

FRAMƎ

THE INTERNATIONAL MAGAZINE OF INTERIOR ARCHITECTURE AND DESIGN > JUL/AUG 2004

Yohji
Yamamoto:
'Are you
crazy?'

Ron Arad:
'Yes. Is
that good
or bad?'

Yamamoto:
'Good.'

www.framemag.com

Belgitudes: The Architect as Troubleshooter
Postcards From Milan
Guerrilla Tactics by Comme des Garçons

EU €15 UK £11 Canada $29.50 Japan ¥2,940 Korea WON35,000 Printed in the Netherlands

About the last edition:

"The best current overview of the creative business in Britain I have seen. It shows an unparalleled and unbiased overview of UK creative excellence, and makes a wonderful resource for creative and design buyer alike."

Graham Peake — Creative Director, TWO design

"Fresh, clean, informative and it does what it says on the label."

Antony Lawrence — Marketing Director, River Design

"The books provide an interesting read and it is useful to see examples of various agencies' creative work covering an array of disciplines in one definitive well presented collection of books."

Steve Bulger — Marketing, JVC UK Limited

"The books are most impressive and excellently produced."

John Graham — Managing Director, AD Creative Consultants

"A beautifully produced directory which enables innovative product designers like LA to remind serious design buyers that they need excellent products if they are to promote their Brand effectively."

Will Bentall — Managing Director, London Associates

"We thought the publication was very stylish, and that the general profile of the contributors was excellent."

Steve La Bouchardiere — Managing Director, Design LSM

"It is an excellently put together and a most interesting set of documents. I am sure it will prove to be extremely useful."

Dave Davies — Graphic Designer, Aramak

"A great showcase of the best in British design and an invaluable reference."

Lance Bates — Manager Marketing Operations, Toyota (GB) PLC

British Design 2004-2005

Branding and Graphic Design
Packaging Design
New Media Design
Interior, Retail and Event Design
Product Design

British Design
2006
Call for Entries

The next edition of this survey of leading British design agencies and studios is scheduled for publication in the autumn of 2006. It will provide the most comprehensive profile of design in this country, offering clients both in the UK and abroad an essential guide to design services in Britain.

Get your portfolio on the design buyer's desk!

A direct mailing campaign covering the UK and the Benelux offers a very persuasive pre-subscription discount. It targets approximately 20,000 design buyers and professionals in marketing, advertising and public relations.

In addition, 1,000 design buyers within a broad range of industrial, commercial and cultural sectors will receive a complimentary copy of the volume. The list of companies will be made available to the participating design agencies.

Be part of it and don't let your name be left out!

If you are a designer or design agency located in the UK and are interested in having your showcase profile in the next edition, please contact us.

Contact our sales manager Marijke Wervers at BIS Publishers for information on closure dates, conditions and how to submit your work.

Marijke Wervers can be reached at: marijke@bispublishers.nl or
T + 31 (0) 20 524 75 68

A.D. Creative Consultants
The Royal Victoria Patriotic Building
Trinity Road / London SW18 3SX
T +44 (0)20 8870 8743 / F +44 (0)20 8877 1151
hello@adcreative.co.uk
www.adcreative.co.uk

Alembic Design Consultants
1 Hanover Yard / Noel Road / London N1 8YA
T +44 (0)20 7288 4580 / T +44 (0)7973 416 261
jmiller@alembic.co.uk
www.alembic.co.uk

Arapaho Communications Limited
Parson's Barn / Main Street / Long Compton
Warwickshire CV36 5LJ
T +44 (0)1608 684 841 / F +44 (0)1608 684 849
info@arapaho.co.uk
www.arapaho.co.uk

Accrue* Corporate Reporting
282 Waterloo Road / London SE1 8RQ
T +44 (0)20 7902 7277 / F +44 (0)20 7928 5136
corporate.reporting@accrue.info
www.accrue.info

Aukett Limited
2 Great Eastern Wharf
Parkgate Road / London SW11 4TT
T +44 (0)20 7924 4949 / F +44 (0)20 7978 6720
Email@aukett.com
www.aukett.com

automatic
Top Floor / 100 De Beauvoir Road
London N1 4EN
T +44 (0)20 7923 4857
speak@automatic-design.com
www.automatic-design.com

BDP Design
16 Brewhouse Yard
Clerkenwell / London EC1V 4LJ
T +44 (0)20 7812 8000 / F +44 (0)20 7812 8399
m-cook@bdp.co.uk
www.bdpdesign.co.uk

Beacon Creative Ltd
No 1 Church Street
Tyne Bridge Approach / Gateshead NE8 2AT
T +44 (0)191 478 4411 / F +44 (0)191 478 7711
info@beaconcreative.com
www.beaconcreative.com

Blackburn's Ltd
16 Carlisle Street / London W1D 3BT
T +44 (0)20 7734 7646 / F +44 (0)20 7437 0017
caroline@blackburnsdesign.com
www.blackburnsdesign.com

Bloom Brand Design
25 The Village
101 Amies Street / London SW11 2JW
T +44 (0)20 7924 4533 / F +44 (0)20 7924 4553
harriet@bloom-design.com
www.bloom-design.com

Blue River
The Foundry / Forth Banks
Newcastle upon Tyne NE1 3PA
T +44 (0)191 261 0000 / F +44 (0)191 261 0010
simon@blueriver.co.uk
www.blueriver.co.uk

Boxer
St Philip's Court / Church Hill
Coleshill / Birmingham B46 3AD
T +44 (0)1675 467 050 / F +44 (0)1675 465 288
paul@boxer.uk.com
www.boxer.uk.com

Also at: Brand Building / 14 James Street
London WC2E 8BU

Brewer Riddiford Design Consultants
69 Shelton Street / London WC2H 9HE
T +44 (0)20 7240 9351 / F +44 (0)20 7836 2897
george@brewer-ridd.co.uk
www.brewer-riddiford.co.uk

Budding
67 Poplar Road / Earlsdon
Coventry CV5 6FX
T +44 (0)24 7671 4805
info@buddingdesign.com
www.buddingdesign.com

Checkland Kindleysides Ltd
Charnwood Edge / Cossington
Leicester LE7 4UZ / Leicestershire
T +44 (0)116 2644 700 / F +44 (0)116 2644 701
marketing@checkind.com
www.checkind.com

cl design
21 Main Road / Underwood
Nottinghamshire NG16 5GP
T +44 (0)1773 530 355 / F +44 (0)1773 533 823
info@cldesignltd.com
www.cldesignltd.com

Creative Edge
Riverside House / Heron Way
Newham / Truro / Cornwall TR1 2XN
T +44 (0)1872 260 023 / F +44 (0)1872 264 110
mail@creativeedge.co.uk
www.creativeedge.co.uk

Dalziel and Pow Design Consultants
5-8 Hardwick Street / London EC1R 4RG
T +44 (0)20 7837 7117 / F +44 (0)20 7837 7137
info@dalziel-pow.co.uk
www.dalziel-pow.co.uk

dare!
3 East Causeway Close
Leeds LS16 8LN / West Yorkshire
T +44 (0)113 281 7080 / F +44 (0)113 281 7088
dare.smt@virgin.net
dareonline.co.uk

Design Bridge
18 Clerkenwell Close / London EC1R 0QN
T +44 (0)20 7814 9922 / F +44 (0)20 7814 9024
enquiries@designbridge.com
www.designbridge.com

Singapore Office:
5 Kadayanallur Street
Singapore 069183 / Singapore
T +65 6224 2336 / F +65 6224 2386
enquiries@designbridge.com
www.designbridge.com

Amsterdam Office:
Keizersgracht 424
1016 GC Amsterdam / The Netherlands
T +31 (0)20 520 6030 / F +31 (0)20 520 6059
enquiries@designbridge.com
www.designbridge.com

Design LSM
The Bath House / 58 Livingstone Road / Hove
Brighton BN3 3WL / East Sussex
T +44 (0)1273 820 033 / F +44 (0)1273 820 058
emily@designlsm.com
www.designlsm.com

Dew Gibbons
49 Tabernacle Street / London EC2A 4AA
T +44 (0)20 7689 8999 / F +44 (0)20 7689 9377
itsgreat@dewgibbons.com
www.dewgibbons.com

Enterprise IG
11-33 St John Street / London EC1M 4PJ
T +44 (0)20 7559 7000 / F +44 (0)20 7559 7001
enquiries@enterpriseig.com
www.enterpriseig.co.uk

Etu Odi Design
4 Pear Tree Court / London EC1R 0DS
T +44 (0)20 7689 9222 / F +44 (0)20 7689 9235
info@etuodi.co.uk
www.etuodi.co.uk

Fitch
121-141 Westbourne Terrace / London W2 6JR
T +44 (0)20 7479 0900 / F +44 (0)20 7479 0600
agoodall@fitchlondon.com
www.fitch.com

Fluid
1/222 The Custard Factory
Gibb Street / Birmingham B9 4AA
T +44 (0)121 693 6913 / F +44 (0)121 693 6911
drop@fluidesign.co.uk
www.fluidesign.co.uk

Front Page Design
26 Woodside Place / Glasgow G3 7QL
T +44 (0)141 333 1808 / F +44 (0)141 333 1909
jackie@frontpage.co.uk
www.frontpage.co.uk

FUSEBOXDESIGN Ltd
St Nicholas Chare
Newcastle upon Tyne NE1 1RJ / Tyne & Wear
T + 44 (0)191 245 7101 / F + 44 (0)191 245 7111
info@fuseboxdesign.co.uk
www.fuseboxdesign.co.uk

Gensler
Roman House
Wood Street / London EC2Y 5BA
T +44 (0)20 7330 9600 / F +44 (0)20 7330 9630
info@gensler.com
www.gensler.com

Hemisphere Design & Marketing Consultants
Binks Building / 30-32 Thomas Street
Northern Quarter / Manchester M4 1ER
T +44 (0)161 907 3730 / F +44 (0)161 907 3731
post@hemispheredmc.com
www.hemispheredmc.com

Hothouse Product Development Partners
Unit 1 College Fields Business Centre
Prince George's Road / London SW19 2PT
T +44 (0)20 8687 2093 / F +44 (0)20 8646 1822
studio@hothouse-design.com
www.hothouse-design.com

Hurricane Design Consultants Ltd
32 Cambray Place / Cheltenham GL5O 1JP
T +44 (0)1242 222 860 / F +44 (0)1242 216 768
david@hurricanedesign.com
www.hurricanedesign.co.uk

IDa
Studio 5 Moira Furnace
Moira / Derbyshire DE12 6AT
T +44 (0)1283 229 998 / F +44 (0)1283 229 909
studio@idadesign.co.uk
www.idadesign.co.uk

Indigo Partnership International
35a Laitwood Road
London SW12 9QN / Balham
T +44 (0)20 8772 0185 / T +44 (0)7801 688 957
F +44 (0)20 8772 0561
kevin@indigopartners.co.uk
www.indigopartners.co.uk

Infinite Design
56 Leazes Park Road
Newcastle upon Tyne NE1 4PG
T +44 (0)191 261 1160 / F +44 (0)191 261 2111
enquiries@infinitedesign.com
www.infinitedesign.com

jones knowles ritchie
128 Albert Street / London NW1 7NE
T +44 (0)20 7428 8000 / F +44 (0)20 7428 8080
info@jkr.co.uk
www.jkr.co.uk

Kiwi
96 Broad Street / Birmingham B15 1AU
T +44 (0)121 688 8881
birmingham@kiwi.co.uk
www.kiwi.co.uk

2 Millharbour / Docklands / London E14 9TE
T +44 (0)20 7750 9940
london@kiwi.co.uk
www.kiwi.co.uk

Landesign
7 Blake Mews / Kew
Richmond-upon-Thames TW9 3QA / Surrey
T +44 (0)20 8332 6699 / F +44 (0)20 8332 6095
info@landdesignstudio.co.uk
www.landdesignstudio.co.uk

Lloyd Northover
2 Goodge Street / London W1T 2QA
T +44 (0)20 7420 4850 / F +44 (0)20 7420 4858
neil.hudspeth@lloydnorthover.com
www.lloydnorthover.com

Loines Furnival
9 Abbey Square / Chester CH1 2HU
T +44 (0)1244 310 456 / F +44 (0)1244 311 044
sara.sartorius@l-f.co.uk
www.loines-furnival.co.uk

Lunartik
Studio 4 / 9 Carisbrooke Rd
Birmingham B17 8NN
T +44 (0)7967 803 909
matt@lunartik.com
www.lunartik.com

Mansfields
Bentalls / Pipps Hill Industrial Estate
Basildon SS14 3BX / Essex
T +44 (0)1268 520 646 / F +44 (0)1268 526 865
mike@mansfieldsdesign.co.uk
www.mansfieldsdesign.co.uk

Minx Creative
2 Old Library Court
45 Gillender Street / London E14 6RN
T +44 (0)20 7510 1005 / F +44 (0)20 7510 1007
team@minxcreative.com
www.minxcreative.com

MoreySmith
24 Marshalsea Road / London SE1 1HF
T +44 (0)20 7089 1470 / F +44 (0)20 7378 1274
information@morey.co.uk
www.moreysmith.com

David Morgan Associates
10 Broadbent Close
20-22 Highgate High Street / London N6 5JW
T +44 (0)20 8340 4009 / F +44 (0)20 8348 6478
david@dmadesign.co.uk
www.dmadesign.co.uk

Navyblue Design Group
122 Giles Street / Edinburgh EH6 6BZ
T +44 (0)131 553 5050 / F +44 (0)131 555 0707
edinburgh@navyblue.com
www.navyblue.com

Third Floor Morelands
17-21 Old Street / London EC1V 9HL
T +44 (0)20 7253 0316 / F +44 (0)20 7553 9409
london@navyblue.com
www.navyblue.com

The Nest
200 St. John Street / London EC1V 4RN
T +44 (0)20 7689 8344 / F +44 (0)20 7689 8347
info@thenest.co.uk
www.thenest.co.uk

Studio North
6 Bradley Street
Northern Quarter / Manchester M1 1EH
T +44 (0)161 237 5151 / F +44 (0)161 237 5131
creativity@studionorth.co.uk
www.studionorth.co.uk

Odd
Fifth Floor
159-173 St. John Street / London EC1V 4QJ
T +44 (0)20 7663 1790 / F +44 (0)20 7336 8789
believe@thankodd.com
www.thankodd.com

Oliis Design
14a-16a The Arches / Goswell Hill
Windsor / Berkshire SL4 1RH
T +44 (0)1753 857 575 / F +44 (0)1753 857 171
info@oliisdesign.com
www.oliisdesign.com

OPX
51 Hoxton Square / London N1 6PB
T +44 (0)20 7729 6295 / F +44 (0)20 7729 8837
postbox@opx.co.uk
www.opx.co.uk

Osborne Pike
Bath Brewery / Toll Bridge Road
Bath BA1 7DE
T +44 (0)1225 851 551
steve@osbornepike.co.uk
www.osbornepike.co.uk

Oyster Partners Ltd
1 Naoroji Street / London WC1X 0JD
T +44 (0)20 7446 7500 / F +44 (0)20 7446 7555
Luke@oyster.com
www.oyster.com

PDD
85-87 Richford Street / London W6 7HJ
T +44 (0)20 8735 1111 / F +44 (0)20 8735 1133
info@pdd.co.uk
www.pdd.co.uk

Pocknell Studio
Readings / Blackmore End
Braintree / Essex CM7 4DH
T +44 (0)1787 463 206 / F +44 (0)1787 462 122
andrea@pocknellstudio.com
www.pocknellstudio.com

Product Resolutions Ltd
The Royal / 25 Bank Plain / Norwich NR2 4SF
T +44 (0)1603 762 676 / F +44 (0)1603 762 656
design@productresolutions.com
www.productresolutions.com

Pure
4 The Heritage Centre
High Pavement / The Lace Market
Nottingham NG1 1HN / Nottinghamshire
T +44 (0)115 958 2107 / M +44 (0)7989 322 304
F +44 (0)115 950 4948
david@purebydesign.co.uk
www.purebydesign.co.uk

R Design
Studio 3, Church Studios
Camden Park Road / London NW1 9AY
T +44 (0)20 7284 5840 / F +44 (0)20 7284 5849
dave@r-email.co.uk
www.r-website.co.uk

Red Cell Scotland
Thomson House
8 Minerva Way / Glasgow G3 8AU
T +44 (0)141 221 6882 / F +44 (0)141 221 5763
simon_macquarrie@redcellnetwork.com
www.redcellglasgow.com

Reinvigorate
2 Gads Hill / Trimmingham Road
Halifax / West Yorkshire HX2 7PX
T +44 (0)1422 340 055 / F +44 (0)1422 340 055
martin@reinvigorate.co.uk
www.reinvigorate.co.uk

Seachange Creative Partners
The Coda Centre
189 Munster Road / London SW6 6AW
T +44 (0)20 7385 5656
nicky@seachangecreative.com
www.seachangecreative.com

Spin
12 Canterbury Court / 1-3 Brixton Road
Kennington Park / London SW9 6DE
T +44 (0)20 7793 9555 / F +44 (0)20 7793 9666
patricia@spin.co.uk
www.spin.co.uk

Springetts
13 Salisbury Place / London W1H 1FJ
T +44 (0)20 7486 7527 / F +44 (0)20 7487 3033
all@springetts.co.uk
www.springetts.co.uk

Start Creative Limited
2 Sheraton Street / Soho / London W1F 8BH
T +44 (0)20 7269 0101 / F +44 (0)20 7269 0102
jen@startcreative.co.uk
startcreative.co.uk

Taxi Studio Ltd
93 Princess Victoria Street / Clifton
Bristol BS8 4DD
T +44 (0)117 973 5151 / F +44 (0)117 973 5181
alex@taxistudio.co.uk
www.taxistudio.co.uk

Tibbatts Associates Ltd
1 St Pauls Square
Birmingham B3 1QU / West Midlands
T +44 (0)121 236 9000 / F +44 (0)121 236 8705
info@tibbatts.co.uk
www.tibbatts.com

Tin Horse
Pelham House, Pelham Court / London Road
Marlborough SN8 2AG / Wiltshire
T +44 (0)1672 519 999 / F +44 (0)1672 511 811
info@tinhorse.com
www.tinhorse.com

Two by Two
348 Goswell Road / London EC1V 7LQ
T +44 (0)20 7278 1122 / F +44 (0)20 7278 1155
zebra@twobytwo.co.uk
www.twobytwo.co.uk

Watt
Watt UK / Ring Road
West Park / Leeds LS16 6RA
T +44 (0)113 288 3210 / F +44 (0)113 275 6044
info@whatswatt.co.uk
www.whatswatt.co.uk

Watt International / 300 Bayview Avenue
Toronto / Ontario / Canada M5A 3R7
T +1 416 364 9384 / F +1 416 363 1098
contactus@wattinternational.com
www.wattinternational.com

Watt International / 172 John Street
Toronto / Ontario / Canada M5T 1X5
T +1 416 593 7254 / F +1 416 593 7940
contactus@wattinternational.com
www.wattinternational.com

Philip Watts Design
32b Shakespeare Street
Nottingham NG5 2HE / Nottinghamshire
T +44 (0)115 947 4809 / F +44 (0)115 947 5828
sales@philipwattsdesign.com
www.philipwattsdesign.com

Word of
50/52 Church St Ashbourne
Derbyshire DE6 1AJ
T +44 (0)1335 348 288
info@wordof.uk.com
www.wordof.uk.com

Zero Design Limited
The Coach House / Northumberland Street
South East Lane / Edinburgh EH3 6LP
T +44 (0)131 556 1333 / F +44 (0)131 556 3113
nobody@zero-design.net
www.zero-design.net

Publication Data

Publisher
BIS Publishers
Herengracht 370-372
1016 CH Amsterdam
P.O. Box 323
1000 AH Amsterdam
The Netherlands
T +31 (0)20 524 7560
F +31 (0)20 524 7557
E bis@bispublishers.nl
www.bispublishers.nl

Sales Management
Marijke Wervers
marijke@bispublishers.nl

Production Coordination
Rietje van Vreden
rietje@bispublishers.nl

Design
Spin, London
www.spin.co.uk

Layout
Bite grafische vormgeving, Amsterdam

Essay
Corinna Dean, London

Text Revision
Mari Shields, Amsterdam

Database Publishing
Marco Kijlstra/Iticus, Amsterdam

Printing
D2Print Pte Ltd